THE WILL TO LEAD

THE
WILL TO
LEAD

*America's Indispensable Role
in the Global Fight for Freedom*

ANDERS FOGH
RASMUSSEN

BROADSIDE BOOKS
An Imprint of HarperCollins*Publishers*

HarperCollins books may be purchased for educational,
business, or sales promotional use. For information, please
email the Special Markets Department at SPsales@
harpercollins.com.

Broadside Books™ and the Broadside logo are trademarks of
HarperCollins Publishers.

FIRST EDITION

Designed by Fritz Metsch

Library of Congress Cataloging-in-Publication Data
has been applied for.

ISBN 978-0-06-247529-9

16 17 18 19 20   RRD   10 9 8 7 6 5 4 3 2 1

To
Annelise, Marie, and Karoline
Martha, Marcus, and Johannes

CONTENTS

————

Letter from a Friend

To the American people,

Soon, you will elect a new president of the United States. As a foreign citizen, I don't have a vote in that election, but perhaps I have a voice. Coming from Europe, having served as prime minister of Denmark and secretary-general of the North Atlantic Treaty Organization (NATO) and worked closely with the two most recent presidents of the United States, George W. Bush and Barack Obama, I have a clear message and plea to the American people: The world needs a policeman. The only capable, reliable, and desirable candidate for that position is the United States. We need determined American global leadership.

The world is on fire. The Middle East is being torn up by war, terrorism, and humanitarian catastrophes that have forced millions of people to flee. Europe is almost sinking under the refugee burden and internal political division. In North Africa, Libya has collapsed and become a breeding ground for terrorists who are spreading instability throughout the region. In Eastern Europe, a resurgent Russia has brutally attacked and grabbed land by force from Ukraine. China is flexing its muscles against its neighbors around the South China Sea. North Korea is a rogue state that threatens its neighbors and the United States with a nuclear attack.

There is a link between the American reluctance to use hard power and this outbreak of fire. If the United States retrenches and retreats, or even if the world thinks that American restraint reflects a lack of willingness to engage in preventing and re-solving conflicts by using military force if need be, it leaves a vacuum that will be filled by the bad guys. Nowhere is this more evident than in Russia's and President Vladimir Putin's behavior. While Europe and America slept, he exploited the vacuum to launch a ruthless military operation in support of the Assad regime and to present Russia as a global power challenging the United States. In Europe, he is trying to carve out a Russian sphere of influence and establish Russia as a regional power capable of diminishing American influence. And this is what is at stake for the United States: Autocrats, terrorists, and rogue states are challenging the American leadership of an international rules-based order, which was created after World War II and has secured the world an unprecedented period of peace, progress, and prosperity.

The next few years will determine the future world order and America's place in it; and in all probability, it will fall to the next US president to make the crucial decisions that will define that future. We are experiencing an intensified struggle between the forces of oppression and the forces of freedom. If the United States withdraws to concentrate on "nation building at home," the forces fighting against liberal democracy and our way of life will gain ground, and the United States will be faced with stronger foes, weaker friends, and a more insecure world.

We have seen again and again that crises breed crises. Force is still a factor. And if we fail to defend freedom and democracy, the forces of oppression will seize their opportunity. We have seen again and again that appeasement doesn't lead to peace. It just incites tyrants. Any failure to counter oppression will only invite further oppression. That is the lesson of the twentieth century—a lesson we must never forget. So while military action remains the last resort, we must be able to resort to it when we need to—not to wage war but to build peace.

I'm a European classical liberal who has always counted on American leadership. Whenever we needed it in the past, it was there. Now I find myself in the unaccustomed position of exhorting the United States not to abandon its vital role as champion of freedom and guarantor of the global order. I grew up in a small European country, Denmark, which has continually had strong ties to the United States. In my family we have always felt a great gratitude to the United States for the sacrifices that the American people made to liberate Europe from Nazism and protect us against Communism.

My father was a farmer and benefited from the Marshall Plan that President Harry S. Truman launched. From my earliest childhood I remember how my parents were inspired and excited by President John F. Kennedy's leadership and youthful energy. And as a young politician, I traveled to the United States and saw President Ronald Reagan's infectious optimism and firm belief in the supremacy of freedom and capitalism, which finally led to the collapse of Communism and the end of the Cold War. As prime minister, I supported President George W. Bush on Afghanistan and Iraq and his freedom agenda to promote liberty and democracy, and as secretary-general of NATO, I worked with President Barack Obama on Afghanistan and Libya, the reinforcement of our territorial defense in Europe, and reforms of our transatlantic alliance. Throughout, I have been guided by a firm belief that America has an indispensable role in the global fight for freedom.

President Truman showed strong leadership and effective conduct by establishing the world order that for nearly seven decades secured an unprecedented peace, development, and wealth. President Kennedy came to stand as a beacon for the free world with his energetic and eloquent communication. And President Reagan led the United States and the world to the victory of freedom over Communism and oppression by his firm conviction of American exceptionalism. Hopefully, future US presidents will combine President Truman's effective *conduct*, President Kennedy's inspiring *communication*, and President Reagan's firm *conviction*. This would prepare the ground for strong American global leadership and a better and safer world.

The United States is an exceptional nation, not in the sense that Americans are necessarily better than other people in the world, but it is an undeniable fact that the United States occupies an exceptional position in the world. When it comes to size and strength, the United States is unmatched as the world's only superpower with a global reach. But even more important, the colonization, creation, and development of the United States and its mature, solid democratic institutions are truly exceptional. America is the inspiring flame of freedom, "the shining city on the hill" that people from all over the world feel attracted by and would like to live in. But that exceptionalism comes with exceptional obligations and responsibilities to defend and promote the principles upon which our free societies are built: individual liberty, democracy, and the rule of law. If America chooses not to intervene early in crises and support the friends of freedom, it will end up having to intervene later, when the enemies of freedom begin to strike at American interests. America is destined to lead. The ancient Greeks believed that you cannot escape your destiny and that the gods will punish you if you try. America should heed the advice of the ancients, play its role as a global leader with conviction, and avoid the unnecessary pain and suffering that come with resisting your destiny. America cannot escape its fate.

I have dedicated this book to our six grandchildren: our American grandchildren, Annelise, Marie, and Karoline, and our Danish grandchildren, Martha, Marcus, and Johannes. Living on both sides of the Atlantic, they are a testament to our strong personal transatlantic bond, and hopefully they will grow up in a secure world where freedom and democracy will prevail over oppression and autocracy thanks to determined American leadership.

With all my best wishes,
Anders Fogh Rasmussen

THE WILL TO LEAD

CHAPTER I

AT THE TIPPING POINT

The only thing necessary for the triumph
of evil is for good men to do nothing.
—*attributed to* EDMUND BURKE

Our world has reached the tipping point.

What began as a pro-democracy uprising in Syria has become a tornado of conflict, sucking regional and global powers into an accelerating cycle of violence. The Islamic State terrorist group has carved out a massive power base across Syria and Iraq, and is battling to expand it. Iran and Saudi Arabia are fighting a proxy war for regional dominance; the terrorist groups al-Qaeda and Hezbollah are trying to carve out their own spheres of control; Russia is using Syria as a stage on which to posture as a superpower reborn and challenge American dominance.

The effects have already reached far beyond the shores of the Mediterranean and the streets of Damascus. Islamic State bombs have caused carnage in Paris and Istanbul, Beirut and Brussels; jihadist groups inspired the San Bernardino and Orlando shooters to commit the deadliest terror attacks on US soil since 9/11. The conflicts in the Middle East have sent millions of people fleeing into Europe, straining to the breaking point the continent's ability to take them in. Russia's Syrian power play provoked the most dangerous armed clash since the Cold War, when a Russian jet violated the airspace of NATO member Turkey and was shot down.

In Syria and Iraq, Yemen and Libya, the body of the state as we know it has collapsed, and hostile powers are gathering like vultures to pick over the remains. Not since the Balkans a century ago has one region held so much potential for global disaster. Shia against Sunni, Russia against Turkey, Iran against Saudi Arabia, Islamic State against the West: Any one of these contests could provide the flash point for a global conflagration.

In this age of interconnections, it has become a cliché to talk of the "global village." Right now, the village is burning, and the neighbors are fighting in the light of the flames. We need a policeman to restore order; we need a fireman to put out the fire; we need a mayor, smart and sensible, to lead the rebuilding.

We need America to play all these roles. No other country in the world can do it. Russia is obsessed with rebuilding the empire the Soviet Union lost; China is still primarily a regional actor; Europe is weak, divided, and leaderless; the old powers of Britain and France are simply too small and exhausted to play the global role they once did. Only America has the material greatness to be able to stop the slide into chaos; only America has the moral greatness to do it, not for the sake of power but for the sake of peace.

And yet right now, the call for isolationism in the United States is growing louder by the day. More and more politicians and commentators are giving in to the temptation that the twin bulwarks of the Atlantic and Pacific have always offered: the temptation to say, "Let the world out there do what it wants; we can pull back the troops, pull up the drawbridge, and be safe."

This is a terribly dangerous philosophy because it is so wrong. History has shown time and again that the bulwarks of the oceans are no defense against a hostile and aggressive world. Imperial Germany proved it in 1917; imperial Japan did it again in 1940; al-Qaeda did it on 9/11. The main thing that has changed since then is the rise of the Internet, with all the dangers of radicalization and cyber-crime that it offers. It would be hard to argue that this has made the world a safer place.

The same way we talk about the global village, we talk about the "international order." For most of us, it is an order that has dominated our whole lives. It has become a shared ideal, a shared dream: The idea that nations can, and should, work together for the greater good. The idea that there are rules that apply to all nations, the great as well as the small. The idea that some rights and values are universal—freedom, democracy, the dignity of the individual. The idea, in the compelling words of the preamble to the United Nations Charter, that all nations should stand together "to save succeeding generations from the scourge of war, which twice in our lifetime has brought untold sorrow to mankind, and to reaffirm faith in fundamental human rights, in the dignity and worth of the human person, in the equal rights of men and women and of nations large and small."

Yet that order is neither an ideal nor a dream: It is a system of rules that was created out of the wreckage of World War II thanks to American leadership. America was the father of the international order; America was its champion in the darkest days of the Cold War; America held the pillars of the world steady when the Soviet Union collapsed, allowing the former Soviet countries to find their place in the international order peacefully.

And now it appears that America is in danger of stepping back and allowing the pillars of the world to crumble. When Russia illegally annexed Crimea in March 2014—the first gunpoint landgrab in Europe since the end of World War II— Secretary of State John Kerry called it an "unbelievable act of aggression" and went on, "You just don't, in the twenty-first century, behave in nineteenth-century fashion by invading another country on a completely trumped-up pretext."

As a statement of principle, this is admirable, but as a guide to policy, it is dangerously naive, because whether it was believable or not, it happened. The problem is exactly that many countries in the world *are* acting in a nineteenth-century fashion: Russia and China are not the only ones, simply the biggest. And when the world's largest country and the world's most populous country seem bent on treating their neighbors in a thoroughly nineteenth-century fashion, the world's most powerful country badly needs a clearer policy than "You just don't do that." The twenty-first century's rules are only as good as twenty-first-century nations' willingness to enforce them; and if the United States cannot be bothered to enforce them, who will?

Indeed, the current foreign-policy debate in the United States is truly frightening for those of us in the twenty-first-century world who believe in the rule of law. On both sides of the US political spectrum, politicians are railing against "free riders" and against "paying for other people's security"; they are dismissing NATO as an unnecessary cost, and foreign engagement as a pointless effort.

These commentators seem bent on dragging America down the wrong road—a dead-end road that looks attractive at the start but hides incalculable pitfalls just around the corner. In the age of globalization, they want to shut the United States off from the globe; in the age of international cooperation, they argue for a retreat into isolation. They want to close the door and tell the rest of the world to go away, but the rest of the world has a tradition of ignoring such warnings.

As a former prime minister of Denmark, I would love it if my country were a superpower, capable of enforcing the rules, but we are not. We are no free riders; we have always done our bit, but we can only work as part of an international team. We cannot be its captain.

We need America to be the captain, to lead and inspire our societies, so that we defend, together, the principles of democracy and individual liberty, the rule of law, and the freedom of trade. If America makes a wrong turn, it is those principles that will suffer, and the cost of reimposing them in ten or twenty years' time will be an order of magnitude greater than the cost of defending them.

Yes, some countries do act in nineteenth-century fashion, and only America can rally the twenty-first-century world in defense of the rule of law. Of course, intervention is neither simple nor easy. The United States has made mistakes in the past; this book will discuss some of them. But my belief is that the only fatal mistake is to turn away from the world and pretend that its problems are not America's problems. Whenever the United States steps back, the actors of evil are emboldened to step forward. In the words attributed to the eighteenth-century British statesman Edmund Burke, "The only thing necessary for the triumph of evil is for good men to do nothing."

A century ago, in the Balkans, the world reached its tipping point, and the result was the most disastrous and destructive war that history had ever seen. Now, in the Middle East, we have reached the tipping point again. Only strong, determined American leadership can stop the international community from falling into the abyss. America needs to shake off the appearance of hesitancy, which has dogged it over the past eight years, and take the lead with renewed energy.

This book is my plea for US leadership, and it falls into three parts. The remainder of this chapter will examine the cauldron of the Middle East and how we got to this tipping point, through a mixture of good intentions, bad decisions, and misunderstood communications. The next three chapters will examine the careers of three US presidents—Harry S. Truman, John F. Kennedy, and Ronald Reagan—who exemplified US leadership on the global stage. The concluding chapters will examine the debate between isolationists and realists, and explain why, and how, America must take the lead to uphold the international order that she did so much to build.

When America Steps Back

There is no easy way to describe the upheavals that have shaken the wider Middle East and North Africa since the beginning of pro-democracy demonstrations in Tunisia at the end of 2010. Almost without exception, the traditional regimes, power structures, and even borders of this vast region have been swept away on a wave of bloodshed. Libya has collapsed; Yemen is on its knees; Iraq and Syria are at the epicenter of the brutal struggle between Shia and Sunni, Iran and Saudi Arabia. Farther afield, Afghanistan is clinging by its fingernails over the precipice of civil war.

These conflicts are so chaotic and wide-ranging that it is hard enough to explain them, let alone extinguish them. They have been fueled by struggles between and within tribes and families as well as nations; they have been driven by religion and the deepest cynicism; they have led to the proclamation of holy states—caliphates—that are built on the profits of slavery, narcotics, torture, and extortion. But I cannot rid myself of the belief that they have one thing in common, and that is that these conflicts took off when the United States stepped back. It is as if American engagement is a lid clamped down on bubbling cauldrons of violence and chaos, and once the lid is off, the cauldron boils over.

It has become customary among America's enemies to blame the United States for all the troubles of the world. According to their narrative, the US campaign in Afghanistan began that country's descent into bloodshed; the US-led invasion of Iraq sparked the fires that are raging there now; and the NATO-led operation in Libya, in which the United States played a crucial role, was what destroyed that country.

In fact, the opposite is true. Every one of those interventions was necessary and justified—in Afghanistan, to close down the terrorist safe haven that the Taliban had given the 9/11 plotters; in Iraq, to stop Saddam Hussein from flouting the will of the international community and defying the United Nations; in

Libya, to stop Mu'ammar Gadhafi from massacring his own people. The anarchy did not begin when America sent the troops in; it began when America pulled the troops out.

The first of those decisions chronologically was the decision to end our NATO-led Afghan combat mission, which we made in late 2010. I was deeply involved in that decision as secretary-general of NATO, a post that I had taken up in 2009. Throughout the early months of my mandate, it became more and more clear to me that the NATO member countries were growing increasingly war-weary. In order to maintain their support for the mission in the short term, it was necessary to set up a clear perspective, goal, and timetable for our mission in the medium term. At the NATO summit in Lisbon in 2010, we therefore decided that the NATO-led International Security Assistance Force (ISAF) operation in Afghanistan should cease by the end of 2014, and responsibility for security would gradually be transferred to the Afghan security forces.

No one argued to prolong our presence in Afghanistan. Afghan president Hamid Karzai complained about the night raids and received a rather robust answer from German chancellor Angela Merkel. But all participants were so eager to leave Afghanistan that I had to caution a bit, saying that the process would be condition-based, not calendar-driven. "We have to make sure we don't leave Afghanistan prematurely," I said.

At the time, this decision was carried by its own political logic: It was essential to emphasize that we were not in Afghanistan as occupiers, and it met an Afghan desire to be masters in their own house. We also needed to preserve NATO's own unity and make sure that there was no talk of a "rush for the exit": The Dutch had already pulled out of Uruzgan province, and there were fears that others might follow, shattering our cherished principle of "in together, out together."

But in retrospect, it was a mistake to let the withdrawal of troops be calendar-driven rather than driven by conditions on the ground. By the end of 2014, the Afghan security forces were not yet fully capable of taking over complete responsibility for security throughout the country. They needed more time, but that was not something the Lisbon agreement allowed.

In short, when NATO and partner combat troops left Afghanistan, they left behind a job that was only partly finished, a task that the Afghan forces were not capable of finishing on their own. The rising tide of violence in Afghanistan since then is the indirect consequence of our decision in Lisbon, well intentioned but ill judged, to end our combat mission by the last day of 2014, whether or not there remained an enemy to fight.

If Afghanistan shows the dangers of what happens when international help withdraws too soon, Libya shows the dangers of what happens when it arrives too late. The NATO-led air and sea campaign for Libya remains, to this day, one of the most effective military operations ever carried out: seven months of air strikes with unprecedented precision that minimized civilian casualties and collateral damage. It saved tens of thousands of lives from almost certain destruction, and it enabled the Libyan opposition to overthrow one of the world's worst and longest-ruling dictators.

However, the political follow-up to the military operation was no less than a disaster. I had expected the UN to lead determined efforts to help the new authorities in Libya. After the fall of the Gadhafi regime, the new political leaders in Tripoli were faced with the daunting task of building new government institutions and a new security system from scratch. But no one was there to help them. The UN resolutions did not allow NATO to have troops on the ground: Once the air mission was completed, we had no choice but to leave. Some people have called this an excuse; it is nothing of the sort. Does anyone seriously believe that a single NATO member would have been willing to occupy Libya illegally, without a UN mandate? We had to wait for the UN to decide what sort of international support was needed.

But the UN did not step into the breach. The truth is that no master plan for the rebuilding of Libya existed, and no urgency was given to the task of drawing one up. And while the UN dithered, the countless factions in Libya took the law into their own hands. It was not just anarchy but anarchy with AK-47s. Soon, the security situation deteriorated and it became almost impossible for international institutions to deploy people and resources to the country. In a crowning irony, at length the then Libyan prime minister asked NATO to help build new Libyan security forces, but before we could send help he resigned, and nobody in Libya was willing to repeat the offer. Now Libya has descended into the abyss. It is a tragic example of the consequences when the international community fails to act—and the tragedy is that it did not have to happen. The chance was there to build Libya anew, but nobody took it.

The Need to Lead

This is not to say that the United States could, or should, have tried to carry out the stabilization of Libya by itself. But my experience has been that the United States has a unique ability to make things happen, to rally international support, and to forge international consensus. No other country has a similar combination of political, diplomatic, economic, and military capabilities. Put bluntly, the United States can make things happen in a way that no other country can—but only when it is willing to lead from the front.

In that regard, the most disastrous message to come out of Washington in 2011 was undoubtedly the notion that the United States had entered a phase of "leading from behind." As a concept, leading from behind makes no sense: If you are not in front, you are not leading—you are either following others or hiding behind them. And as a policy, it simply doesn't work, because the people you claim to be leading will either stop and wait for you to overtake them or go off in their own direction. The American president must lead from the driver's seat.

The term "leading from behind" appeared in an article in the *New Yorker* on May 2, 2011, and was attributed to "an adviser" to the president. It has never been officially embraced by the administration, and I have never heard the president or any of his secretaries use that expression. But the mere fact that it was disseminated, though anonymously, sent an unfortunate signal to those wicked forces that were looking for new chances to fill the vacuum left by a hesitant sheriff. It was interpreted as meaning that, after masterminding the withdrawals from Afghanistan and Iraq, the United States had no intention of getting involved in yet more overseas missions—in other words, that the forces of chaos and oppression could commit as many atrocities as they liked, and America would let them get away with it.

It is only fair to point out that the distaste for foreign intervention in the wake of the Afghan and Iraqi wars was by no means limited to America. I well remember a meeting of NATO foreign ministers I chaired as secretary-general of NATO in December 2012. The Syrian civil war had been raging for over a year; we knew that government forces had been attacking civilians indiscriminately, even firing Scud missiles. I argued that it was time for the world's greatest military alliance to begin "prudent planning" for all eventualities in Syria—so that if international action was judged to be necessary, we could act swiftly and decisively. But apart from a few ministers, including Secretary of State Hillary Clinton and British foreign secretary William Hague, there was little support for this proposal. On the contrary, there was a strong pushback from a number of other ministers. I still remember a foreign minister from one of the major European countries who argued vigorously against even thinking of prudent planning. He also asked his ambassador to make the same point to me separately, and even took hold of me the next morning to be sure that I did not start any kind of prudent planning.

I had to shelve the plan, since all decisions in NATO require unanimity, but it was to my regret, because I believe that it is the essence of a security organization like NATO to be prepared for all eventualities. I had not proposed a specific action, but only prudent—that is to say, very discreet—planning: When even that was excluded, it tells a lot about the distaste for intervention that predominated.

The phrase "leading from behind" changed the whole tone of the debate. If it had never been spoken, the narrative might have been of a general Western reluctance to act. Once it was spoken and published, it became the prism through which all foreign-policy decisions during Obama's presidency were viewed. Thus, the 2010 decision to withdraw from Afghanistan, the 2011 withdrawal of US troops from Iraq, and the 2012 decision not to enforce the White House's "red line" on the use of chemical weapons in Syria were woven into a narrative that claimed, in essence, that Obama had given up on foreign policy and foreign military action, and that the most he would ever do was to "lead from behind"—if he acted at all.

I have no doubt that the decisive moment in this narrative was President Obama's decision not to strike Syria in 2013. Early in the conflict, President Obama declared that the use of chemical weapons would be a "red line," which would trigger US action. On a number of occasions, chemical attacks were reported, but were judged not to have been on a scale that would constitute crossing the red line. However, on August 21 of that year, chemical munitions were fired from Syrian government–held territory into the small but strategically located town of Ghouta, on the outskirts of Damascus. Human rights organizations and journalists on the ground reported gruesome scenes: deaths of men, women, and children consistent with chemical attacks, possibly sarin gas. It was estimated that more than a thousand people were killed.

At last, Obama declared that the line had been crossed. American forces moved into position, ready to strike; French and British forces moved up to support them (although the British Parliament then refused to sanction British action). The world held its breath, waiting for an American strike. It never came. At the last minute, literally on the eve of taking action, Obama changed his mind. He called off the strikes and offered a diplomatic way out if Assad would get rid of his chemical weapons. First Russian president Putin, and then Assad himself, agreed to the deal, and a UN Security Council resolution was passed authorizing the UN and the Organization for the Prohibition of Chemical Weapons (OPCW) to mount an operation to dismantle Syria's chemical stockpile. Just over two weeks later, the UN/OPCW team was on the ground receiving reasonable cooperation from Syria, and while we cannot be sure that all chemical weapons were actually declared and removed from Syria, the great majority appear to have been.

In terms of chemical weapons it was an effective move, but in terms of the bigger picture it was a disaster. In the eyes of the world, Obama had gone eye to eye with Assad, and it was Obama who had blinked. This, more than anything else, gave the impression that America simply would not take action in the Middle East, no matter what the provocation—and that emboldened both Assad and Putin.

In an interview with the *Atlantic*, President Obama has thrown more light on his motives. Four years earlier, the president believed, the Pentagon had "jammed" him on a troop surge for Afghanistan. Now, on Syria, he was beginning to feel jammed again. In addition to this, he had four concerns. He stated that the first and most important factor was "our assessment that while we could inflict some damage on Assad, we could not, through a missile strike, eliminate the chemical weapons themselves, and what I would then face was the prospect of Assad having survived the strike and claiming he had successfully defied the United States, that the United States had acted unlawfully in the absence of a UN mandate, and that would have potentially strengthened his hand rather than weakened it." Second, "I had come into office with the strong belief that the scope of executive power in national-security issues is very broad, but not limitless." Third, he would not fire a shot, as long as there were UN inspectors on the ground in Syria. And fourth, it played a role that Prime Minister David Cameron had not been able to find a parliamentary majority for British participation in a possible joint action.

Whatever his motives were, there is no doubt that the decision not to strike Syria had a crucial, serious, and lasting impact on America's credibility among both friends—France and traditional allies in the region—and foes. In Congress as well as in the administration, the president fell out with those who had previously supported a tough and consistent line. America's enemies saw new opportunities in the American hesitation, among them Russian president Putin. The conclusion is clear: Once the US president says he will strike, you have to strike. There is no choice.

It seems to me that President Obama was aware of the political costs: "And so for me to press the pause button at that moment, I knew, would cost me politically. . . . I believe ultimately it was the right decision to make." Jeffrey Goldberg, who interviewed Obama for the *Atlantic*, calls August 30, 2013, Obama's "liberation day," the day when he defied the foreign-policy establishment and its cruise-missile playbook.

If August 30, 2013, really is perceived as Obama's liberation day, it bodes no good for the rest of his presidential term. For I believe that this day could be remembered as the day he let the Middle East slip from America into the hands of Russia, Iran, and the Islamic State (IS). In fact, by 2013, America's enemies felt confident that she no longer wanted to lead. The world's policeman had gone into retirement.

Reality versus Perception

That perception had dire consequences on the ground. I am convinced, for example, that the reason President Putin annexed Crimea and launched an undeclared war in Ukraine and a declared one in Syria is that he thought the United States would let him get away with it. In the same way, I believe that Iran made such an aggressive push into Syria and Yemen because it thought the Obama administration only cares about the 2015 nuclear accord. Fear of American power has always been the one overwhelming factor that kept a lid on these countries' geopolitical ambitions. Now, rightly or wrongly, that fear has disappeared.

The narrative that President Obama is somehow a soft or inactive president does not entirely square with the facts. When the US military called for a troop surge in Afghanistan in 2009, he provided it; when NATO allies demanded action over Libya in 2011, he made sure that the US military provided the capabilities that the other allies simply did not have. He ordered US Special Forces into Pakistan to take Osama bin Laden; he greatly increased the use of targeted drone strikes; he launched air strikes against IS in 2014, enabling Kurdish forces on the ground to retake much of the territory lost to the group.

Nevertheless, it is clear that, for Obama, military action is only something that he will take reluctantly, and after all other options have been obviously exhausted—and that has emboldened America's foes. Perhaps unsurprisingly in a president who was elected on the promise to end the wars in Afghanistan and Iraq, he has been the most vocal president since Jimmy Carter in his opposition to the early use of military force. In what was arguably his defining foreign-policy speech, delivered at West Point on May 28, 2014, President Obama outlined what could be called his "last resort" doctrine on the use of military power: "Since World War II, some of our most costly mistakes came not from our restraint, but from our willingness to rush into military adventures without thinking through the consequences."

He made the point even clearer in his State of the Union speech on January 20, 2015, when he stated, "When the first response to a challenge is to send in our military, then we risk getting drawn into unnecessary conflicts."

Let me stress that I have no quarrel with Barack Obama. I regard him as an insightful and sincere political leader with strong personal integrity and a belief in justice, the rule of law, and a rules-based international order. And on a personal level, my relationship with Obama is the very best. After all, he was instrumental in getting me elected NATO secretary-general in 2009, and it was Barack Obama who, over a midwestern specialty—a root beer float—in Chicago in 2012, asked me to extend my mandate as secretary-general for another year. I am not the guy who turns his back on colleagues with whom I have collaborated closely, and throughout my mandate I had the very best cooperation with the president and his team.

Nor do I doubt that President Obama, in his demonstration of restraint, is in line with a large portion of the American population. Surveys from the Pew Research Center show that a majority of Americans believe that the United States is doing too much, rather than too little, to help solve the world's problems, and a majority agree that "the US should mind its own business internationally and let other countries get along the best they can on their own." Other surveys, including the annual Chicago Council Surveys, indicate that while a majority of Americans are in favor of the United States playing an active role in world affairs, there is also a long-standing public aversion to the use of military force. Thus, Obama's own preference for focusing on domestic issues clearly reflects that of most American voters. This is wholly understandable; after all, politicians are elected, first and foremost, to look after their own countries, not other people's.

This noninterventionism sentiment pops up regularly in both political parties. Since President Herbert Hoover and the prominent senator Robert Taft in the 1930s, there has also been a strong noninterventionism movement in parts of the Republican Party. While it was marginalized under the leadership of President Reagan and Presidents George H. W. Bush and George W. Bush, it has resurfaced in recent years, and you will often hear noninterventionist, even isolationist-like, speeches from the right wing of the Republican Party, including the Tea Party groups. So President Obama is not the only one to represent this foreign-policy thinking. It is rooted in American history, in political traditions, and in the inmost sentiments of many Americans.

However, noninterventionism, not to speak of isolationism, is a troubling approach in today's world. We live in an era of civil wars, ethnic conflicts, insurgency, and terrorism, which will drag on for many years. There are, of course, many reasons for this political upheaval: Resurgent and rising states are looking for conquest rather than compromise. Autocrats are seeking to hold on to power, whatever the cost. Ideological and religious extremists and fanatics will take any opportunity to spread their creed and kill for it. And the most challenging aspect about such extremists is that they mistake restraint for weakness and become encouraged by it. In fact, the problem facing the United States is this: It is not enough for America to be strong or to play the role of world leader. The United States has to be *seen* to be strong and to be playing the leader's role.

It is that need for visible, determined leadership that lies at the heart of this book.

Toward a New American Leadership

To have to play the part of leader of the free world is a hard, and perhaps unfair, calling. No other leader, no other country in the world, faces such a challenge. But the way America's enemies work makes it inevitable. Autocrats and terrorists are tempted to test their room for maneuver and the determination of the free world, and in particular the United States, if they sense they can carry out their illegal and heinous acts without serious consequences. If the United States retreats or is perceived to retreat, a vacuum will be left that will be filled by the "bad guys."

Recent history is sadly full of such examples. While there may be many good reasons why the United States has refrained from interfering directly in the Syrian civil war, the US absence likely weakened the moderate opposition to the Assad regime and strengthened the extremists, creating space for President Putin. While the threat of air strikes against Syria after Assad's use of chemical weapons eventually ended with the regime agreeing to let the chemical weapons be destroyed, the failure to act more strongly in defense of President Obama's "red lines" sent a dangerous signal to both Damascus and Moscow about hesitant and wobbling US leadership.

While the US withdrawal from Iraq in 2011 can be explained, the American absence most likely created space for more sectarianism, paved the way for IS, and indeed tempted Putin to seek rapprochement with Iraq. While the United States made a crucial contribution to NATO's successful air operations in Libya, the American absence in the post-conflict period most likely hampered the new Libyan authorities' reconstruction of the country and created a breeding ground for extremism, terrorism, and sectarian conflicts and violence. While there were good reasons for the American rebalancing from Europe to Asia and the "reset" with Russia after the end of the Cold War, the diminished American presence in Europe is likely to have given Putin an appetite for more room to maneuver and an expansion of the Russian sphere of interest.

Because of America's strength and dominant global position, all powers and actors in the world orient themselves with reference to the great superpower. Allies detect American firmness and evaluate America's steadfastness. Adversaries are lying in wait for signs of growing or fading clout or resolve. When the United States looks to retrench and retreat, her allies will be concerned while her opponents will see new opportunities.

The global village needs a policeman, and over the past hundred years, it has been shown time and again that the United States is the only state capable of acting in that capacity. When America is willing to step forward and defend the rules-based order that it did so much to create, the results are peace and stability. When America steps back, the world's actors of ill will think they can break the rules and get away with it, and the result is conflict and chaos.

Over the past two decades, the world has changed fundamentally. What has not changed is its need for stability, security, and peace. Only the United States can provide that; and so I believe that the next US president will need to articulate a new foreign-policy doctrine, to guide the free world through the new era in which we live. That doctrine will have to set out more clearly than ever before the concept of American leadership.

It is a role that other presidents have played before. Harry S. Truman shaped the world after the wreckage of World War II, as a master of effective *conduct*. John F. Kennedy faced down the greatest danger ever to threaten the West, as a master of inspiring *communication*; Ronald Reagan brought the Cold War to a bloodless end through his *conviction* in the American people and the American Way. The new president must aspire to the standards of these outstanding leaders if he, or she, is to stop the fires of chaos from spreading and, ultimately, put them out.

The goal of this book is to set out why the world still needs American leadership and what it should look like. But first, we will turn to three pivotal presidents, Truman, Kennedy, and Reagan, and examine how they steered their country through times that were as challenging as our own.

CHAPTER 2

HARRY S. TRUMAN

American Leadership and Effective Conduct

We are facing a bunch of thugs, and the only theory a
thug understands is a gun and a bayonet.
—SENATOR HARRY S. TRUMAN

O ne man deserves more credit than any other for laying
the foundations of our modern world: the thirty-third
president of the United States, Harry S. Truman.
Truman is a deeply paradoxical character: a leader and visionary
who tried to bridge the divide between and within his country's
political parties, yet left office as the least popular president
America has ever seen. He steered the Western world through
the end of World War II and the outbreak of the Cold War. He
led the United States, and the free world, in responding to the
Soviet blockade of Berlin and the North Korean invasion of the
South; he oversaw both the bombing of Hiroshima and Nagasaki and the founding of the United Nations. In the United
States, he is remembered for the woeful approval ratings with
which he left office. But he deserves to be remembered as the
man who paved the way for the rise of liberal democracy, despite all the challenges from authoritarian forces.

Thanks to Truman's leadership in America, and American leadership in the world, the half-century following World War II saw the United States successfully establish, protect, and advance a liberal order, carving out a vast free world within which an unprecedented era of peace and prosperity could flourish in Western Europe, East Asia, and the Western Hemisphere.

Although tensions between the United States and the Soviet Union sometimes rose to dangerous levels, the period was characterized, above all, by a lack of direct armed conflict between the great powers. While local and regional conflicts occasionally developed into delimited proxy wars, including two hugely costly wars in Asia, the United States and the Soviet Union overall kept the Cold War cold. Just as important, the American presence in Europe and East Asia put an end to the cycles of war that had torn both regions since the late nineteenth century.

The number of democracies in the world grew dramatically. The international trading system expanded and deepened. Much of the world enjoyed unprecedented prosperity. The Western model was largely successful—so much so that the Soviet empire finally collapsed under the pressure of the West's political and economic success. The liberal order expanded to include most of the rest of Europe and much of Asia.

All of this was the result of many forces: the political and economic integration of Europe, the success of Japan and Germany, and the rise of other successful Asian economies. But none of it would have been possible without a United States willing and able to play the abnormal and unusual role of preserver and defender of a liberal world order, and a US president willing to lead from the front.

———

HARRY S. TRUMAN grew from a modest background to become one of the greatest American presidents. He was born in Lamar, Missouri, in 1884. Although the young Harry was an excellent student, his parents could not afford to send him to college, and following his high school graduation Truman worked at a variety of jobs, including farming, oil drilling, and banking. He opened a haberdashery shop that eventually went bankrupt. After failing in the haberdashery business, Truman decided to seek a political career, serving as a county official from 1922 until his election to the US Senate in 1934. He was to serve as a senator for the next decade.

Growing up in modest circumstances had a significant effect on Truman's whole character and behavior. He was known as a plain and blunt-spoken man of the people. Some of the phrases he coined passed into everyday speech and have remained current to this day: "The buck stops here," "If you can't stand the heat, get out of the kitchen," and "It sure is hell to be president." While his main interest as a senator was in domestic issues, his foreign-policy focus and attitudes intensified as Nazism and Fascism gained ground in Europe and Asia during the 1920s and 1930s.

During the First World War, Truman served in the American Expeditionary Forces, which were deployed to Europe after the United States entered the war in April 1917. The experience of the twentieth century's first great man-made catastrophe had a lasting impact on him.

Sent to France with the National Guard of Missouri, Truman served as commanding officer of a field artillery battery. Captain "Harry" was highly regarded by the nearly two hundred men of Battery D under his command. In his great Truman biography, David McCullough describes how Captain Truman worked his men hard, "insisting on strict behavior, making them 'walk the chalk' (stick to the straight line of discipline), and driving himself no less." McCullough writes that Truman transformed what had been generally considered the worst battery in the regiment to what was clearly one of the best. On a personal level, Captain Truman was a friendly and obliging man. He took a personal interest in his men and would talk to them in a way most officers would not. McCullough quotes one of Truman's men: "Harry had such warmth and a liking for people. He was not in any way the arrogant, bossy type, or Prussian type of officer." While under Truman's command in France, Battery D did not lose a single man.

The war was a transformative experience for Truman in three ways: leadership, attitude toward Germany, and world-view. Truman had entered military service in 1917 as a family farmer with very little education and a record of unsuccessful business ventures behind him. But during the war he achieved a positive record and acquired valuable leadership skills that benefited his political career after the war.

Truman's active military service in Europe contributed greatly to shaping his view of the world and America's inter-national role. He experienced firsthand the horrors of war, and these experiences contributed to his negative attitude toward Germany, which he viewed as the aggressor. But first and foremost, Truman became more of an internationalist than most of his compatriots. His participation in the war and stay in Europe had given him an international outlook that came to characterize his political career. While his constituents at home in Missouri tended to be mildly isolationist, Truman cautiously followed President Roosevelt's internationalism. In the 1930s, Senator Truman voted for the Neutrality Act, which severely impaired the ability of the United States to help the Allies in Europe. However, this vote was more an expression of a calculated, pragmatic, and tactical maneuver to satisfy the traditional isolationist tendencies in Missouri than a reflection of Truman's true attitudes. His speeches, especially in the late 1930s, showed that he feared the spread of Fascism and Nazism, and that he believed the United States needed to be prepared.

In a speech in Larchmont, New York, in 1938, he warned that "conditions in Europe have developed to a point likely to cause an explosion any time." He called for the establishment of an air force "second to none," arguing that no one could be more mistaken than the isolationists, and that America had erred gravely by refusing to sign the Versailles Treaty and refusing to join the League of Nations. His condemnation of this policy was fierce, portraying it as a moral failure: "We did not accept our responsibility as a world power." In Truman's eyes, America could not pull back and hide from the world. America was blessed with riches and wanted peace, but "in the coming struggle between democracy and dictatorship, democracy must be prepared to defend its principles and its wealth." In a letter to one of his constituents in early 1941, he explained why America might review her noninterference policy, stating with typical bluntness, "We are facing a bunch of thugs, and the only theory a thug understands is a gun and a bayonet."

In retrospect, this period in which he struggled against the deep-seated urge toward isolationism can be seen as having defined his future vision and policies. Indeed, for the American isolationists, the 1930s were the high-water mark of their political dominance. The 1930s witnessed the rise of Nazism and Fascism in Germany, Japan, Italy, and Spain; the Japanese invasion of Manchuria in 1931; Adolf Hitler's rise to power in 1933; Benito Mussolini's invasion of Ethiopia in 1935; Germany's remilitarization of the Rhineland and the German and Italian intervention in the Spanish Civil War in 1936; Japan's invasion of central China in 1937; Hitler's absorption of Austria, followed by his annexation and conquest of Czechoslovakia in 1938 and 1939. None of these events was considered a reason for the United States to get involved. Even after the Nazi and Soviet invasions of Poland and Finland in 1939 and the Nazi crushing of traditional US allies such as France, the Netherlands, Belgium, Luxembourg, Denmark, and Norway in 1940, it was still the dominant view that the United States shouldn't get involved. A prominent and leading isolationist, the Republican senator Robert Taft, argued that the United States should not range "over the world like a knight-errant, protecting democracy and ideals of good faith, and tilting, like Don Quixote, against the windmills of fascism." Truman found himself in strong opposition to the isolationist senators.

The Japanese attack on Pearl Harbor in 1941 was a wake-up call: a reminder that even the world's greatest power is not protected by two large oceans. The Japanese attack and Hitler's subsequent declaration of war led to America's full-scale entry into the war in both Europe and Asia.

But even before that attack, it was clear to the administration of President Franklin D. Roosevelt that American inactivity could not be sustained forever. In his annual message to Congress on January 6, 1941, Roosevelt presented his case for American involvement, arguing for continued aid to Great Britain and greater war production at home. In helping Britain, Roosevelt stated, the United States was fighting for the universal freedoms that all people possessed. He spoke about "the four freedoms"—freedom of speech, freedom of worship, freedom from want, and freedom from fear. As America entered the war, these four freedoms became the lighthouse for American political leaders and the American people.

The recognition of the need for a strong American involvement in world affairs to defend American security interests was reflected in the Atlantic Charter, a pivotal policy statement that Roosevelt drafted together with British prime minister Winston Churchill in the fall of 1941. Churchill had been appointed prime minister in 1940. A staunch and outspoken opponent of the appeasement policy that had been pursued unsuccessfully by the British government led by Prime Minister Neville Chamberlain during the 1930s, Churchill had the moral authority and rhetorical power to rally his country against the Nazis in a way that no other leader could have done. But after the fall of France in June 1940, Great Britain was in a desperate situation, standing alone in Europe against triumphant tyranny, bearing the full brunt of Hitler's air war, and living with the daily threat of invasion. Churchill was determined to obtain assistance from the United States. However, President Roosevelt had severe difficulties in winning political acceptance for assistance to the British. The isolationists were quick to insist that the United States should avoid being involved in a foreign entanglement that could lead to American engagement in the war. Churchill alternately begged and encouraged the Americans to help in the fight against the Nazis. In a radio address, he ended the broadcast with an explicit message to Roosevelt with a heartfelt plea: "Give us the tools, and we will finish the job."

Roosevelt was responsive and intensified contacts with the embattled British prime minister. In August 1941, Churchill and Roosevelt met off the coast of Newfoundland, aboard their respective warships, to formulate a common strategy, although the United States would not officially enter the war until four months later. The objectives of the war were conveyed in the Atlantic Charter. The charter included President Roosevelt's four principles and stated the ideal goals of the war: no territorial aggrandizement; no territorial changes made against the wishes of the people; self-determination; restoration of self-government to those deprived of it; reduction of trade restrictions; global cooperation to secure better economic and social conditions for all; freedom from fear and want; freedom of the seas; and abandonment of the use of force, as well as the disarmament of the aggressor nations.

The Atlantic Charter set goals for the postwar world and inspired many of the international agreements that shaped the world thereafter. It guided US and British policy in the years of war that followed, as they fought back against the forces of tyranny in the Pacific, the Atlantic, North Africa, and Europe. It provided the underpinning of values that cemented their sometimes troubled alliance; it inspired the soldiers who fought their way from the beaches of Normandy to the banks of the Rhine and the Elbe, from the ridges of Papua New Guinea to the beaches of Saipan and Iwo Jima.

It also inspired Truman, who at that time headed the

Truman Commission investigating fraud in defense contracts. It was a position that brought him to nationwide prominence, and Roosevelt tapped him as his vice presidential running mate in 1944. It was one of Roosevelt's last major decisions. On April 12, 1945, Roosevelt died, and after less than three months as vice president, Harry S. Truman was sworn in as the thirty-third president of the United States. Truman told reporters, "I felt like the moon, the stars, and all the planets had fallen on me." Certainly the weight of the world's shattered economies and societies was about to do so.

———

ONE OF TRUMAN's first decisions as president was also one of the hardest. Victory in Europe was declared just weeks after he took office, but the war against Japan was still dragging bloodily on. An urgent plea to Japan to surrender was rejected. Truman ordered atomic bombs dropped on cities devoted to war work. Hiroshima and Nagasaki were blasted into history as the first-ever casualties of atomic weapons. Japanese surrender quickly followed. After six years of war, many millions of casualties, and billions of dollars in war spending, Germany, Japan, and their allies had been defeated. The question that Truman dedicated the next eight years to answering was how to make sure that such a global conflagration could never happen again.

It is tempting to argue that an earlier American engagement and stronger American global leadership in the 1930s could have prevented war. That was certainly the conclusion that Roosevelt and Truman drew. Would-be aggressors had to be deterred before they became too strong to be stopped short of all-out war.

Or, as Roosevelt put it, the task for America was to "end future wars by stepping on their necks before they grow up."

It was not easy to follow in the footsteps of the highly regarded Roosevelt, but Truman overcame low expectations. He established a reputation at home for personal integrity, honesty, and efficiency. On the international stage, he strove to create a solid foundation of international organizations, structures, norms, and rules in the military, political, and economic fields to prevent future devastating wars, preserve peace, and provide progress and prosperity.

From the perspective of the early twenty-first century, it is clear that this strong network of international institutions was one of the main reasons that the postwar world recovered relatively quickly and embarked on an era of peace, growth, and abundance. The institutions reduced the postwar chaos and made up for the lack of trust among states. They helped reduce member states' fear of one another, a crucial factor in the aftermath of the devastating world war. International institutions provided a forum for negotiation among states. They provided continuity and a sense of stability. They fostered cooperation among states for their mutual advantage.

Truman's commitment to international institutions proved beneficial for the United States and the world. The alternative would have been a multipolar anarchy. During the Cold War, the world was characterized by a bipolar power balance between the United States and the Soviet Union. The American-led international institutional system helped foster stability and economic progress within the non-Communist world; and after the collapse of the Soviet Union and international Communism, the established institutional framework helped facilitate a quick integration of the former Communist states into the already established international system and thus contributed to the stabilization of the new world order.

Among some conservatives in America, multilateral institutions are considered an impediment to American influence and leadership. Actually, the opposite is true. Thanks to the international system that was established under American leadership after World War II, the United States has been able to promote and protect the values and interests of the free world. In a very real sense, by championing international cooperation based on the balance of powers, rules, and responsibilities, Truman shaped the free world in America's image, and the free world was better for it.

Truman backed up his commitment to multilateral institutions with the leadership and management skills he had learned in the trenches. If his aims were visionary, his policies were concrete, detailed, and highly effective. Four of his initiatives stand out as the key pillars of the international order to this day.

First was the establishment of the United Nations. Based on the negative example of the League of Nations, a weak and ineffective body that the United States never joined, Truman took the lead in establishing a new, stronger international organization, the United Nations. Signed in San Francisco in 1945, the UN Charter merged two forms of international decision making. The UN would implement collective security through the Security Council, designating five major powers as permanent members wielding veto power, together with a rotating group of ten additional countries. The Security Council was vested with special responsibility to maintain international peace and security. The General Assembly would be universal in membership and based upon the doctrine of the equality of states—one state, one vote.

While the UN Security Council has often been paralyzed due to the veto power of the five permanent members, the UN has proved useful as the only international forum where all the world's nations, irrespective of their political system, can meet, discuss, and possibly make decisions. Born in California and housed in New York, the UN carries in its very bones Truman's dedication to the international order.

Second, America also led the way in setting up a new global economic system. The 1930s had seen a progressive fragmentation of the international economy as nation after nation resorted to protectionism; World War II had seen the wholesale destruction of much of the world's industrial base. To put that system back on a sustainable footing, 730 delegates from all forty-four Allied nations gathered at the Mount Washington Hotel in Bretton Woods, New Hampshire, while the war was still raging, to hold the United Nations Monetary and Financial Conference, also known as the Bretton Woods Conference.

Their goal was nothing less than to agree on a system of rules, institutions, and procedures to regulate the international monetary system so that it could never again be pulled apart by aggressive governments. To meet that goal, they established the International Monetary Fund (IMF) and the International Bank for Reconstruction and Development, which today is part of the World Bank. In order to facilitate a global free-trade system, they established the General Agreement on Tariffs and Trade (GATT) in 1948.* They saw rules-based trade and the unhindered flow of capital as the keys to worldwide prosperity. That vision is just as true today. The Bretton Woods institutions have helped stabilize fragile states and the global economy, and facilitated global trade and economic cooperation; even China has chosen to work within this established international order. It is no coincidence that the IMF was one of the prime responders in the great financial crisis of 2009 onward. The effectiveness and representative nature of the institution may have been called into question by some, but no serious critic has questioned its importance. If it had not existed, we would have had to invent it in the middle of the crisis. It is thanks to Truman that we did not have to.

Third, in order to protect Western Europe against the military threat from an assertive Soviet Union, the United States, Canada, and ten Western European countries created the North Atlantic Treaty Organization (NATO) in 1949. The devastated nations of Western Europe were too weak to defend themselves, so America provided the ultimate unilateral security guarantee: a shelter under its nuclear umbrella. The core of their transatlantic commitment was the pledge that an attack on one alliance member will be considered an attack on all. In another indication of the importance of US leadership, they signed their founding treaty in Washington, DC. NATO is the bedrock

---

* In 1994 GATT was replaced by the World Trade Organization (WTO), an intergovernmental organization that regulates international trade by providing a framework for negotiating trade agreements and a dispute resolution process aimed at enforcing participants' adherence to WTO agreements.

of Euro-Atlantic security, and, thanks to NATO, Europe has experienced the longest period of peace in the history of the continent.

Finally, the Truman administration advanced a series of crucial initiatives to create growth and jobs, prevent social unrest on the ruined European continent, and prevent Communism from getting a foothold among the poverty-stricken and disenchanted European peoples.

One such example was the Greek-Turkish aid program. Launched in March 1947, it provided economic assistance to Turkey and to the Greek government in their fight against Communism. Turkey and Greece were seen as the linchpin of security in the Mediterranean and Middle East. Until 1947, they had been funded by Britain, but the postwar empire was no longer able to keep up its payments.

The most important initiative, however, was launched by Secretary of State George C. Marshall in a speech to the graduating class at Harvard University on June 5, 1947, three years almost to the day after US, British, Canadian, and Allied troops stormed ashore in Normandy and brought the fight against Hitler back to Western Europe. Marshall called for a comprehensive program to rebuild Europe. Fanned by the fear of Communist expansion and the rapid deterioration of European economies, Congress passed the plan in March 1948 and approved funding that would eventually rise to over $12 billion for the rebuilding of Western Europe, or some $130 billion in current dollars.

The Marshall Plan stimulated European industrialization and brought extensive investment into the region. It was also a stimulant to the US economy by establishing markets for American goods. It is rightly viewed as the foundation of modern Europe's prosperity. Later, the Europeans embarked on an integration process that led to the establishment of institutions that eventually became the European Union. This regional cooperation underpinned the international order that was established under American leadership.

But the most significant feature of the Marshall Plan and the Greek-Turkish aid program was the new, engaged policy they embodied, and which Truman articulated in a historic address to Congress on March 12, 1947. While the policy of re-engagement began with Roosevelt, it was Truman who became its champion, and whose name was ultimately attached to it as the *Truman Doctrine.*

In his pivotal speech, Truman vowed that the United States would provide political, military, and economic assistance to all democratic nations under threat from external or internal authoritarian forces. The Truman Doctrine effectively reshaped US foreign policy, turning it away from its long-held stance of avoiding regional conflicts not directly involving the United States, to one of possible intervention in faraway conflicts. In a stroke of rhetorical genius, Truman elevated engagement to a moral choice directly affecting every single American citizen, because it was based on American values:

> I believe that it must be the policy of the United States to support free peoples who are resisting attempted subjugation by armed minorities or by outside pressures. I believe that we must assist free peoples to work out their own destinies in their own way.

And why should the United States take that stance? Truman's answer remains just as true today as it did nearly seventy years ago:

> The seeds of totalitarian regimes are nurtured by misery and want. They spread and grow in the evil soil of poverty and strife. They reach their full growth when the hope of a people for a better life has died. We must keep that hope alive. The free peoples of the world look to us for support in maintaining their freedoms. If we falter in our leadership, we may endanger the peace of the world, and we shall surely endanger the welfare of our own nation.

For Truman there was no difference between Fascism and Communism. He detested any form of totalitarianism, and he made his anti-Communism clear in his inaugural on January 20, 1949:

> Communism is based on the belief that man is so weak and inadequate that he is not able to govern himself, and therefore requires the rule of strong masters. Democracy is based on the conviction that man has the moral and intellectual capacity, as well as the inalienable right, to govern himself with reason and justice. Communism subjects the individual to arrest without lawful purpose, punishment without trial, and forced labor as the chattel of the state. It decrees what information he shall receive, what art he shall produce, what leaders he shall follow, and what thoughts he shall think. Democracy maintains that government is established for the benefit of

the individual, and is charged with the responsibility of protecting the rights of the individual and his freedom in the exercise of those abilities of his. . . . Communism holds that the world is so widely divided into opposing classes that war is inevitable. Democracy holds that free nations can settle differences justly and maintain a lasting peace. . . . I state these differences . . . because the actions resulting from the Communist philosophy are a threat to the efforts of free nations to bring about world recovery and lasting peace.

In retrospect, these observations seem self-evident, because we have seen the bankruptcy and collapse of the Soviet Union and Communism. But we must remember that the situation was radically different by the end of the 1940s. The Soviet Union was seen as a strong nation with global ambitions to spread Communism to the rest of the world. And indeed, Communist dictatorships were established in Eastern and Central European countries, under severe pressure and active intimidation from the Soviet Union. Even in the West there was a strong left-wing camp, notably among intellectuals, who admired Soviet Communism. It was in this light that President Truman took up the battle against the "false communist philosophy."

———

IN DOMESTIC POLITICS, the Truman era was characterized by a stalemate between the executive and legislative branches. But he scored some notable legislative achievements in foreign and military policy, despite facing a hostile Congress. Truman tapped into the experiences of his ten years in the Senate to forge relationships with members of Congress at a difficult time. A Democratic president facing a Republican Congress and a divided Democratic Party, Truman stands as a model for other presidents during periods of divided government. His decisive leadership reoriented American politics, economics, and foreign relations. In terms of foreign policy, Truman made some of the most crucial decisions in US history, setting a high standard for American global leadership and engagement. He founded a new world order through a new global economic system; a new transatlantic security alliance; a comprehensive economic recovery plan, notably the Marshall Plan for Europe; and the United Nations, though it had been prepared by his predecessor.

Truman also made some difficult decisions, none more so than the decision to use atomic weapons against imperial Japan. This was a controversial and widely disputed decision—perhaps the most far-reaching decision that any elected leader anywhere has ever had to make. On August 9, 1945, after Nagasaki was bombed, Truman made a public statement on why the atomic bombs were used: "We have used it against those who attacked us without warning at Pearl Harbor, against those who have starved and beaten and executed American prisoners of war, against those who have abandoned all pretense of obeying international laws of warfare. We have used it in order to shorten the agony of war, in order to save the lives of thousands and thousands of young Americans." Truman and his generals had been appalled by the sacrifices made by Japan's death-or-victory soldiers and the losses they had inflicted on the United

States in defending islands such as Saipan. The thought of the deaths they would inflict if the Japanese homeland were invaded was too much to be accepted as long as any other option remained open—even the unthinkable.

In 1948, Truman recognized the new State of Israel. It was another controversial decision, partly made against the counsel of some of his advisers, who argued that it would antagonize Arab states and jeopardize American access to oil. While initially somewhat skeptical about the establishment of a Jewish state, Truman declared that he would handle the situation in the light of justice, not oil. He saw it as an act of humanity. The murder of six million Jews by the Nazis had been the worst atrocity of all time. A strong personal sympathy for the Jewish cause and an outrage at the plight of Jewish refugees post-Holocaust made Truman firm in his position to allow the Jewish people their own home: Israel.

Nazism and Japanese imperialism were defeated, but it did not mean an end to conflict—nor an end to the need for decisive American leadership. In 1948, the Soviets blockaded the western sectors of Berlin in an attempt to push the West out of Berlin, cutting all surface traffic to West Berlin. A desperate Berlin, faced with starvation and in need of vital supplies, looked to the West for help. The Americans created a massive airlift to supply Berliners until the Soviets backed down one year later. Berlin became a symbol of President Truman's and the United States' resolve to stand up to the Soviet threat.

In June 1950, when the Communist government of North Korea attacked South Korea, Truman promptly decided to do whatever had to be done to meet this aggression. War followed from 1950 to 1953, and the Americans succeeded in keeping the Communists at bay. In an address on July 19, 1950, President Truman once again outlined his view on American global responsibility:

> By their actions in Korea, Communist leaders have demonstrated their contempt for the basic moral principles on which the United Nations is founded. This is a direct challenge to the effort of the free nations to build the kind of world in which men can live in freedom and peace. This challenge has been presented squarely. We must meet it squarely . . . the fact that Communist forces have invaded Korea is a warning that there may be similar acts of aggression in other parts of the world. The free nations must be on their guard, more than ever before, against this kind of sneak attack. . . . We know that the cost of freedom is high. But we are determined to preserve our freedom—no matter the cost.

Truman's foreign program was to combat Communist expansion and to strengthen what he called the "free world." Supported by leading Republicans, this policy became bipartisan in its major aspects. Backed by American economic and atomic power, it was remarkably successful. The Truman Doctrine was the turning point in damming Soviet and Communist expansion because it put the world on notice that it would be American policy to support the cause of freedom wherever it was threatened.

President Truman left office as the most unpopular president in American history, but he demonstrated a brilliant example of American leadership and effective conduct in building a new international order after World War II. More than any other individual, he deserves to be remembered as the architect of the international order in which we live and are struggling to preserve.

———

WHILE TRUMAN'S INTERNATIONALISM is indisputable, views vary on whether his policy of active engagement in the world was a break with or a natural continuation of the American foreign policy tradition. One view of history emphasizes American isolationism. This school of thought typically quotes George Washington's Farewell Address: "It is our true policy to steer clear of permanent alliances with any portion of the foreign world." Other favorite reference points include John Quincy Adams's famous statement that America "goes not abroad, in search of monsters to destroy" and Thomas Jefferson's warning against "entangling alliances."

Historians who emphasize the isolationist tradition typically view Theodore Roosevelt as the first internationalist president, followed by Woodrow Wilson and then Franklin Roosevelt and Harry Truman. An alternative view, however, notes that the United States has always been a strongly internationalist and universalist nation motivated by a deep sense of mission beyond narrow geographical boundaries. Robert Kagan advances this interpretation of history persuasively in his book *Dangerous Nation*, arguing that "the pervasive myth of America as isolationist and passive until provoked rests on a misunderstanding of America's foreign policies in the seventeenth, eighteenth, and nineteenth centuries."

Kagan shows that the American founding generation was, in fact, highly internationally oriented and by no means isolationist. In fact, George Washington faced geopolitical realities remarkably similar to the challenges of the twentieth century. In Kagan's interpretation, Washington's warning against permanent alliances was, in fact, a specific and unique attempt to maneuver America away from its alliance with France at a time when French expansionism had become reminiscent of the subsequent German expansionism in the late nineteenth and early twentieth centuries. In both cases, the United States opted to align with Great Britain, reasoning that if a continental power subjugated the British, America would likely be next.

Kagan also draws an interesting parallel to the Cold War in a discussion of Washington's Treasury secretary, Alexander Hamilton:

> Prefiguring the argument advanced a century and a half later by George Kennan about another revolutionary despotism, Hamilton argued that French leaders were driven to expansionism abroad by fear of their own lack of legitimacy at home.

Besides the first president, no other president did as much to shape early American history as did the sixteenth president, Abraham Lincoln, who abolished slavery and kept the Union intact. And like Washington and Hamilton, Lincoln prefigured many of the challenges faced by modern-day decision makers.

During a private visit to Lincoln's hometown of Springfield, Illinois, in September 2009, I came across a powerful quote from Lincoln that I included in a speech that same month at the Atlantic Council in Washington, DC:

> Our defense is in the preservation of the spirit which prizes liberty as a heritage of all men, in all lands, every-where. Destroy this spirit, and you have planted the seeds of despotism around your own doors.

Lincoln spoke these words on a symbolic date: September 11, 1858. Exactly 143 years before the terrorist attacks of 2001, Lincoln already knew what President George W. Bush subsequently described as the key lesson of 9/11: "The human condition elsewhere matters to our national security."

The historical interpretation is important because history often creates a sense of legitimacy that can be influential in present public policy discussions. If one accepts the view that the American founders were isolationists at heart, then it is easy to conclude that Truman's internationalism was an aberration fostered by the unique circumstances surrounding the beginning of the Cold War. Now that circumstances are different, the temptation will be to fall back on the original ideas of the founders if at all possible. If, on the other hand, we believe that America has always been internationalist at heart, then the case for continued internationalism in the present age becomes much stronger.

I personally find Kagan's interpretation of American history very convincing. I believe Truman carried the mantle of Washington and Lincoln, but as we shall see in the next chapter, it fell to another Cold War president to truly rise to the rhetorical level of the Declaration of Independence and the Gettysburg Address.

CHAPTER 3

JOHN F. KENNEDY

Personal Leadership and Inspiring Communication

It was the nation and the race . . . that had the lion's
heart: I had the luck to be called upon to give the roar.
—WINSTON CHURCHILL

He mobilized the English language and sent it into battle.
—PRESIDENT KENNEDY
*on Winston Churchill when he conferred honorary US
citizenship upon the British leader*

On October 22, 1962, in a televised address to the
American people, President John F. Kennedy drew a
clear red line. The background was perhaps the greatest crisis of modern times: The Soviet Union had started to
establish nuclear missiles in Cuba. These missiles would pose a
direct threat to the United States.

In one of the most momentous speeches ever delivered by a
US president, Kennedy served notice to the Soviet leader, Nikita
Khrushchev, that the era of Soviet expansion had reached its end
and that America stood ready to turn back the tide wherever it
should rise again:

Any hostile move anywhere in the world against the
safety and freedom of peoples to whom we are committed,

including in particular the brave people of West Berlin, will be met by whatever action is needed.

It was a remarkable speech, a bravura performance delivered with absolute commitment from the brink of nuclear war, and it worked. In the anxious days that followed, American democracy and Soviet totalitarianism went eyeball to eyeball over the island of Cuba, and it was the Soviet side that blinked.

The Cuban Missile Crisis cemented Kennedy's place in the pantheon of great US and world leaders, but it took a long road to bring him there, and there were false turns and stumbles on the way. How Kennedy arrived at that famous speech, and how he had the courage and conviction to deliver it in a way that convinced Khrushchev to back down, is a lesson for future leaders.

———

IN MID-OCTOBER 1962, KENNEDY had been informed about ongoing construction work to place Soviet nuclear missiles in Cuba—missiles that could strike deep into the United States. Kennedy assembled his closest advisers to consider options and direct a course of action for the United States that would resolve the crisis. Some advisers, including all of the military chiefs, argued for an air strike to destroy the missiles, followed by a US invasion of Cuba. Others favored just firm warnings to Cuba and the Soviet Union. The president decided upon a middle course, and the way he steered it speaks volumes of the leader he had become. Kennedy combined military action, diplomatic pressure, and powerful rhetoric to convey a strong message to both his friends and his enemies.

First, overriding his generals, on October 22 he ordered a naval quarantine of Cuba. A former naval officer himself, he micromanaged the movements of the US Navy, because he realized that the navy's actions were a way to communicate American intentions on a larger scale to the Soviet Union. Meanwhile, preparations for a possible military strike on Cuba proceeded and the readiness of the US military was put on the highest level. That same day, Kennedy sent a letter to Khrushchev, declaring that the United States would not permit offensive weapons to be delivered to Cuba and demanding that the Soviets dismantle the missile bases already under construction or completed and return all offensive weapons to the Soviet Union.

Perhaps most important, Kennedy went public with a stark televised address to America, the Soviet Union, and the world. He delivered a speech that marked his determination to counter the Soviet aggression, to mobilize the American people, and to reassure friends and allies of the American resolve to defend both freedom and peace.

Kennedy put the Cuban Missile Crisis into a historical perspective. He drew on the "lessons from Munich," lessons that he himself had observed on a sweeping visit to Europe almost a quarter of a century before: "The 1930s taught us a clear lesson: Aggressive conduct, if allowed to go unchecked and unchallenged, ultimately leads to war." He warned against inaction, in words that also prepared the American people for possible sacrifice:

Let no one doubt that this is a difficult and dangerous effort on which we have set out. No one can foresee precisely what course it will take, or what costs or casualties will be incurred. Many months of sacrifice and self-discipline lie ahead—months in which both our patience and our will will be tested; months in which many threats and denunciations will keep us aware of our dangers. But the greatest danger of all would be to do nothing.

The tone of his remarks was stark in setting a clear red line:

It shall be the policy of this nation to regard any nuclear missile launched from Cuba against any nation in the Western Hemisphere as an attack by the Soviet Union on the United States requiring a full retaliatory response upon the Soviet Union.

And true to his firm belief in the American responsibility to lead and defend the free world, he concluded:

The cost of freedom is always high, but Americans have always paid it. And one path we shall never choose, and that is the path of surrender or submission. Our goal is not the victory of might, but the vindication of right; not peace at the expense of freedom, but both peace and freedom.

Kennedy's firm stance and rhetoric had an impact. Through secret back channels, the Soviet leader indicated an interest in finding a political solution, and secret negotiations followed. Eventually an agreement was reached between Kennedy and Khrushchev. Publicly the Soviets would dismantle their offensive weapons in Cuba and return them to the Soviet Union, subject to United Nations verification, in exchange for a US public declaration and agreement never to invade Cuba without direct provocation. Secretly, the United States also agreed to dismantle all US missiles deployed in Turkey and Italy against the Soviet Union, but whose presence was not known to the public.

The crisis was over. Most crucially, the world avoided a nuclear disaster. But Kennedy's handling of the crisis also strengthened the position of the United States, weakened the Soviet Union, and put a brake on Soviet endeavors to expand the power and reach of international Communism.

Because the withdrawal of the US missiles from NATO bases in Italy and Turkey was not made public at the time, Khrushchev appeared to have lost the conflict and become weakened. The perception was that Kennedy had won the contest between the superpowers and Khrushchev had been humiliated. Thus, by communicating clearly and managing his military forces closely, Kennedy delivered a political and diplomatic defeat to the Soviets while avoiding a dangerous military escalation that could have ended in nuclear war.

During the Cuban Missile Crisis, Kennedy showed the ability to match inspiring words with convincing deeds. He demonstrated what happens when the American president acts from a position of strength, and is perceived as strong and determined in his leadership among friends and foes alike. He showed, as Truman had shown, that American global leadership made America stronger, and the world safer. His handling of the Cuban Missile Crisis encapsulated the attitudes his early formative years had shaped and the experience he had gained during the first two years of his presidency. It was Kennedy's key insight that invigorating communication, backed by deeds, is crucial for effective leadership. The president of the United States must communicate both vision and policies in an inspiring manner, using eloquent rhetoric that convinces the people to follow and leaves friends and foes alike in no doubt about the American resolve—in the words of his inaugural—to "assure the survival and the success of liberty."

Kennedy also realized that appeasement doesn't lead to peace. As Europe had shown so painfully in the 1930s and 1940s, the community of free nations must have the strength and resolve to counter the forces of oppression before it is too late. Therefore, the free world needs a strong leader. The United States must exert strong global leadership to instill hope and inspiration for all people in the world who yearn for freedom, peace, and democracy.

————

ON JANUARY 20, 1961, John Fitzgerald Kennedy was sworn in as the thirty-fifth president of the United States. His inaugural address set out the principles that he had developed as a keen observer of international affairs for more than twenty years, and the lessons of engagement and communication that were at their core. For Kennedy, there was simply no alternative to American leadership, and since Americans could not escape their destiny they might as well embrace it:

> In the long history of the world, only a few generations have been granted the role of defending freedom in its hour of maximum danger. I do not shrink from this responsibility: I welcome it. I do not believe that any of us

would exchange place with any other people or any other generation. The energy, the faith, the devotion which we bring to this endeavor will light our country and all who serve it, and the glow from that fire can truly light the world.

Kennedy truly believed that America was destined to lead. He communicated this belief to the American people, to America's allies, and to America's enemies in powerful speeches time after time. This inaugural address contains what is probably the strongest commitment to American global leadership ever given by a president of the United States:

Let every nation know, whether it wishes us well or ill, that we shall pay any price, bear any burden, meet any hardship, support any friend, oppose any foe, to assure the survival and the success of liberty.

This memorable passage sent an unmistakable message, to both friends and foes, of determined American resolve to bear the special responsibility of the world's leading democracy and to execute global leadership in defense of liberty. The inaugural speech was clearly the speech of the leader of the free world. It was widely praised as eloquent, inspiring, and idealistic, but also firm, crisp, and vigorous. It sent a clear signal to America, and to the world, that a new, youthful, energetic president was prepared to lead the free world.

That resolve was on display, even more strikingly, when Kennedy visited Berlin in 1963. He delivered yet another remarkable speech that boosted the morale of the besieged West Berliners, gave hope to the peoples of Western Europe, and manifested his role as the leader of the free world:

> Today, in the world of freedom, the proudest boast is, "Ich bin ein Berliner." . . . There are many people in the world who really don't understand, or say they don't, what is the great issue between the free world and the Communist world. Let them come to Berlin. . . . Freedom has many difficulties, and democracy is not perfect, but we have never had to put a wall up to keep our people in, to prevent them from leaving us. . . . You live in a defended island of freedom, but your life is part of the main. So let me ask you, as I close, to lift your eyes beyond the dangers of today to the hope of tomorrow, beyond the freedom merely of this city of Berlin or your country of Germany to the advance of freedom everywhere, beyond the wall to the day of peace with justice, beyond yourselves and ourselves to all mankind. . . . All free men, wherever they may live, are citizens of Berlin, and therefore, as a free man, I take pride in the words, "Ich bin ein Berliner."

Among many memorable lines in many memorable speeches, it is perhaps ironic that Kennedy's most famous line was not delivered in English, or in America, but in German, and in Germany. And yet that fact perfectly encapsulates the leader he had become. This was a man who ventured to stand just yards away from Soviet-dominated territory and declare, in the language of the city and country where he was standing, that he was one of them. He invoked the images of freedom and peace, in a way that is still quoted and remembered now, over half a century later. The Berlin speech was the culmination of his political career, and the epitome of American leadership in the world.

Kennedy was of the firm conviction that the key to American global leadership was an economically and technologically strong America. When he became president, the Soviet Union was ahead of the United States in the race for manned flights into space. This worried Kennedy, and in the first televised debate with Vice President Richard Nixon on September 26, 1960, he declared:

> I want people in Latin America and Africa and Asia to start to look to America to see how we're doing things, to wonder what the President of the United States is doing, and not to look at Khrushchev or look at the Chinese communists. That is the obligation upon our generation. . . . I think it's time America started moving again.

Kennedy saw the importance of setting an ambitious goal that would inspire the American people, rallying them to an extra effort to bring the United States in front and to consolidate the global leadership in the defense of freedom. In a special address to Congress on "Urgent National Needs," on May 25, 1961, he outlined the ambition of "landing a man on the moon and returning him safely to the earth." In a speech at Rice University in Houston, Texas, on September 12, 1962, he further elaborated on this vision, emphasizing its contribution to assuring the American leadership:

Those who came before us made certain that this country rode the first waves of the industrial revolution, the first waves of modern invention, the first wave of nuclear power; and this generation does not intend to founder in the backwash of the coming age of space. We mean to be part of it—we mean to lead it. . . . Yet the vows of this nation can only be fulfilled if we in this nation are first, and, therefore we intend to be first. In short, our leadership in science and in industry, our hopes for peace and security, our obligation to ourselves as well as others, all require us to make this effort.

Kennedy's dream came true. The United States was the first nation to land a man on the moon. The US technological edge provided in itself a powerful contribution to the economic supremacy of the free world over the Soviet Union and the world's other Communist nations. But more important, the United States enhanced its political image as an admirable role model and leader of the free world.

Kennedy understood that to carry out global leadership, the US president's communication must be based on strength and vigor. The communication should combine three qualities into a unified, powerful message: the rhetoric itself should be vigorous, appealing, and eloquent; the delivery of the speech should underpin the image of determined leadership through a compelling and dynamic physical appearance; and last, but certainly not least, communication should not just be words but should be backed up with decisive actions and visible leadership.

More than any previous American president, Kennedy was

aware of the need to communicate strength to the rest of the world, and he was the first American president who really understood the power of television as a medium of communication. He took advantage of this medium to the utmost to communicate his message in a striking way, through powerful speeches, interviews, and press conferences. He showed an unprecedented openness to the media and the public and embodied youthfulness, dynamism, and determination. Through countless well-composed and rhetorically elegant speeches, he presented his vision and his politics in a way that inspired the American people and the people of the entire free world, showed leadership and strength, and marked an impassable red line for the aggressive Soviet Union and its Communist allies.

President Kennedy's speeches stand as a landmark demonstration of how inspiring communication can set new goals, create enthusiasm, and mobilize popular support by demonstrating determination, direction, and dynamism.

———

THERE ARE CERTAIN events in Kennedy's life that shaped his character and run all through his words and deeds. His military service in the Pacific during World War II was undoubtedly an experience that was deeply rooted in his mind. In August 1943, Lieutenant John F. Kennedy and the twelve-man crew of a US Navy patrol torpedo (PT) boat were rammed by a Japanese destroyer and sunk. Two crew members were killed; the rest survived. Kennedy showed great courage and determination in the rescue operation. He helped a seriously wounded comrade ashore on a small island by swimming and towing him for several hours. The next day he towed the wounded crew member to a larger island. During the six days they were stranded, he was tireless in his efforts to get help, and showed great physical strength and stamina, leadership and courage.

The PT 109 incident had a great and lasting influence on Kennedy's attitude and thinking. He felt responsible for the two dead crew members. Also, his own elder brother, Joseph, was killed during the war. Obviously, that had a deep impact on both the family and John F. Kennedy personally, and in his political activity he returned repeatedly to the sacrifices that generations of Americans had made for their country. Courage and leadership, responsibility and sacrifice were recurring themes in Kennedy's speeches. The fact that Kennedy had experienced the war firsthand shaped his individual character, his political views, and his governmental actions. The principles upon which he built his attitude toward life were rooted in his personal experiences from a battle of life and death between the forces of oppression and the forces of freedom.

Equally crucial in shaping his character and political attitudes was his trip to Europe in 1939, just before the outbreak of World War II. In the summer of 1939, the world stood on the brink of the greatest war ever fought. The forces of Fascism were rising in Europe and Asia. Hitler and Stalin were feeling their way toward an alliance, with the aim of carving up the young states of Central and Eastern Europe between them. The old democracies of Western Europe were divided and hesitant. Nation after nation felt the threat of the coming conflagration and drew in upon itself, hoping to avoid destruction by appeasing the dictators.

In that most crucial summer, Kennedy made a long visit to

Europe. He stayed at the homes of Polish families. He crossed Eastern Europe by train to Moscow. He visited Prague, Vienna, and Munich, and he arrived in Berlin in August, only a few days before Hitler's invasion of Poland. The climax of his prewar experiences came on September 3, 1939, two days after Hitler launched his blitzkrieg against his eastern neighbor, when he took a seat in the visitors' gallery of the House of Commons and listened to Prime Minister Neville Chamberlain, a leader who had failed to prepare Britain to meet a totalitarian threat, announce that Britain and France were now at war with Germany.

Chamberlain had given Hitler an ultimatum: Leave Poland, or we are at war. Hitler ignored the threat, believing that Britain would cave in over Poland, as it had over his gobbling up of Czechoslovakia in 1938. With a heavy heart, Chamberlain admitted in an address to the British people that the policy of appeasement that he had championed for so long had failed, because Hitler had had no intention of being appeased:

> It would have been quite possible to have arranged a peaceful and honorable settlement between Germany and Poland, but Hitler would not have it. He had evidently made up his mind to attack Poland whatever happened, and although he now says he put forward reasonable proposals which were rejected by the Poles, that is not a true statement. . . . His action shows convincingly that there is no chance of expecting that this man will ever give up his practice of using force to gain his will. He can only be stopped by force.

Addressing a packed House, Chamberlain admitted the ruin of the policy that he had championed:

> Everything that I have worked for, everything that I have hoped for, everything that I have believed in during my public life, has crashed into ruins.

However, Kennedy listened with much greater enthusiasm to one of the members of Parliament who responded to Chamberlain's speech: Winston Churchill, who had endured years of political isolation for his opposition to appeasement. Typical of the man, his speech was both far more upbeat than Chamberlain's and far more eloquent:

> The Prime Minister said it was a sad day, and that is indeed true, but at the present time there is another note which may be present, and that is a feeling of thankfulness that, if these great trials were to come upon our Island, there is a generation of Britons here now ready to prove itself not unworthy of the days of yore and not unworthy of those great men, the fathers of our land, who laid the foundations of our laws and shaped the greatness of our country. This is not a question of fighting for Danzig or fighting for Poland. We are fighting to save the whole world from the pestilence of Nazi tyranny and in defense of all that is most sacred to man. This is no war for domination or imperial aggrandizement or material gain; no war to shut any country out of its sunlight and means of progress. It is a war, viewed in its

inherent quality, to establish, on impregnable rocks, the rights of the individual, and it is a war to establish and revive the stature of man.

In the visitors' box, Kennedy would have been perfectly placed to hear and judge the two men for himself. Winston Churchill was not just a skilled politician and a strong leader. He was also a first-class orator. As a young man, Churchill wrote an essay on the power of oratory, "The Scaffolding of Rhetoric" (1897), in which he ranked rhetoric first among the political virtues, and he practiced it himself to perfection. Usually, people listened with great attention to Churchill's speeches because of their vigor, their vivid imagery and linguistic elegance. It was to a great extent because of his rhetorical skills that Churchill became such a successful and strong leader during World War II and became a symbol of courage and perseverance when Britain was left alone in the struggle against Hitler's Germany.

The respect Kennedy gained for Churchill and his extraordinary rhetoric lasted throughout his life: In 1955, when he was recuperating from back surgery, he lay in bed reading Churchill for several hours every day, and he often echoed Churchill in his own speeches. This has been analyzed brilliantly by Thurston Clarke in his book, *Ask Not: The Inauguration of John F. Kennedy and the Speech That Changed America*. For example, Kennedy employed Churchill's trademark phrase (and the title of the second volume of his monumental war memoirs) when he said in a January 14, 1960, speech to the National Press Club, "We will need in the sixties a president who is willing and able to summon his national constituency to its finest hour." Churchill's resounding response to the fall of France, too, inspired one of Kennedy's own greatest addresses. In a speech to the House of Commons on June 4, 1940, Churchill vowed, "We shall fight on the beaches, we shall fight on the landing grounds, we shall fight in the fields and in the streets, we shall fight in the hills; we shall never surrender." Kennedy was to use that same cadence in his own inaugural address, two decades later. But his vision of Churchill's rhetoric was best expressed by the comment he made twenty-four years later, on April 9, 1963, when he conferred honorary US citizenship upon the British leader: "He mobilized the English language and sent it into battle."

Kennedy was to spend much of his career learning how to mobilize the American language and send it into battle "to establish, on impregnable rocks, the rights of the individual" (Churchill, September 3, 1939).

————

KENNEDY'S BACKGROUND WAS an unlikely one for a man who was to become the undisputed leader of the free world, as much a champion of his generation as Churchill was of his. His father, Joseph Kennedy, was known as a passionate isolationist during his term as US ambassador to Great Britain from 1938 to 1940. Joe Kennedy was opposed to American support for the United Kingdom and opposed to American involvement in the war. He supported Chamberlain's appeasement policy and declared in the *Boston Globe* in November 1940 that "democracy is finished in England."

Yet the son drew different lessons from the events that his

father had witnessed. President Kennedy's inaugural address was a stark showdown with American isolationism. In that respect, it was also a showdown with his own father and a decisive break with his isolationist heritage. That may be the reason why former president Truman reconciled with the new young president. Initially Truman opposed Kennedy's candidacy, probably because he disliked his father, Joseph Kennedy, primarily because of his isolationism. Truman endorsed President Kennedy's inaugural address by telling reporters that history would rank it as one of the greatest inaugurals of all time. "It was short, to the point, and in language anyone can understand," he said. "Even I could understand it, and therefore the people can." In Kennedy's own words, "The torch had been passed on." From Truman to Kennedy, there is a direct line.

———

THOSE WERE DAYS in which the torch of leadership of the free world was sorely needed. At the beginning of 1961, on January 6, Khrushchev had delivered an alarming speech under the headline "For New Victories of the World Communist Movement." In the speech, Khrushchev pledged that the Soviet Union would instigate and support "just wars of liberation" in countries such as Algeria, the Congo, Laos, and Vietnam, and predicted these wars would result in Communist states across the Third World. Khrushchev's aggressiveness unsettled Kennedy, and he was conscious that it would require decisive leadership to counter the threat from the Soviet Union. Yet his first experiences of leadership were anything but assured. Indeed, two initial failures in his foreign and security policy gravely weakened the president in Khrushchev's eyes. These initial mistake shaped greatly Kennedy's approach to leadership and sharpened his awareness of the need to appear as a strong leader. This insight marked the rest of his presidency.

Ironically, the first lesson was taught by Cuba. Kennedy gave the green light to an Eisenhower-initiated invasion of the Bay of Pigs in Cuba in 1961. Kennedy had only been in office two months when he ordered the implementation of a watered-down plan inherited from the Eisenhower administration to topple Cuban leader Fidel Castro. An invasion of Cuba was to be sponsored covertly and carried out by CIA-trained anti-Castro refugees. Assured by military advisers and the CIA that the prospects for success were good, Kennedy gave the go-ahead. In the early hours of April 17, 1961, approximately fifteen hundred Cuban refugees landed at the Bay of Pigs on Cuba's southern coast. The plan appeared to be based on false assumptions, and Castro's forces quickly overwhelmed the refugee force. Moreover, the administration's cover story collapsed immediately. It soon became clear that despite the president's denial of US involvement in the attempted coup, Washington was indeed behind it. The misadventure cost Kennedy dearly and taught him a painful lesson. He failed to critically examine the plan developed by the Central Intelligence Agency and the Pentagon and, as a result, ended up with an operational failure that was painful in and of itself, but even more important, a communication disaster signaling America's lack of resolve.

One might expect that such an operational and communication disaster would have weakened President Kennedy seriously. Yet, he communicated strength in an hour of weakness. In a speech on April 20, 1961, the day after the misfortune, Kennedy made clear that he would profit from that lesson and intensify the struggle against Communist expansionism:

> The message of Cuba, of Laos, of the rising din of Communist voices in Asia and Latin America—these messages are all the same. The complacent, the self-indulgent, the soft societies are about to be swept away with the debris of history. Only the strong, only the industrious, only the determined, only the courageous, only the visionary who determine the real nature of our struggle can possibly survive. . . . I am convinced that we in this country and in the free world possess the necessary resource, and the skill, and the added strength that comes from a belief in the freedom of man. And I am equally convinced that history will record the fact that this bitter struggle reached its climax in the late 1950s and the early 1960s. Let me then make clear as the President of the United States that I am determined upon our system's survival and success, regardless of the cost and regardless of the peril.

At a press conference on April 21, 1961, Kennedy took full responsibility for the management of the failed operation. At a critical question from a journalist, he gave the famous answer: "There is an old saying that victory has a hundred fathers and defeat is an orphan. . . . I am the responsible officer of the government, and that is quite obvious." This satisfied the American people, and Kennedy's ratings in the polls rose.

However, the damage had already been done in terms of reduced Soviet respect for Kennedy. The president was unwilling to involve the American military in a full-scale invasion of Cuba, which Khrushchev mistook for American weakness. Further, his handling of the crisis and its diplomatic fallout gave Khrushchev and his advisers the impression that Kennedy was indecisive, not well prepared for decision making in crisis situations, and, in general, too weak. This impression was reinforced by Kennedy's soft response during the Berlin crisis of 1961, particularly the building of the Berlin Wall.

———

WORLD WAR II ENDED in victory for the Allies but not in freedom: Fascism was defeated, but Communism emerged stronger and more aggressive than ever. Berlin, Hitler's monumental capital, was occupied by the victorious Allies but then divided among them. In 1948, Stalin sought to strangle the free and capitalist West Berlin by cutting off all land access to it; led by Truman, the Western allies responded with a yearlong airlift that kept Berlin alive until the Soviet blockade ended.

But the problem of Berlin lingered. West Berlin remained under Western control but it was located deep inside East German territory, and that made its protection from Communist takeover a constant challenge for the Western powers. At the same time, the mere existence of West Berlin was increasingly becoming a burden for the Soviet Union and the Communist regime in East Germany. The divided city was increasingly a demonstration of the difference between Communism and capitalism, with West Berlin and West Germany as free, prosperous, and thriving communities, while East Germany lagged behind because of lack of freedom and the inherent inefficiency of the Communist system. More and more East Germans chose to leave the East and settle in the West.

For the United States, West Berlin's political freedom and economic success were clear symbols and convincing demonstrations of the superiority of the free, democratic, and capitalist system. The United States was strongly committed to defend West Berlin's freedom and independence, so a Soviet decision to cut off the land corridor to West Berlin once again would trigger a serious confrontation between the two powers.

In 1958, Khrushchev delivered a speech in which he demanded that the Western powers—the United States, Great Britain, and France—pull their forces out of West Berlin within six months. This ultimatum sparked a three-year crisis over the future of the city of Berlin that culminated in 1961 with the building of the Berlin Wall. Berlin, which Kennedy had visited in 1939, was to leave an indelible mark on his presidency.

In the summer of 1961, Kennedy met with Khrushchev in Vienna to address the ongoing issue of Berlin. However, they did not find any solution to the Berlin problem, and Khrushchev prepared to take his own form of action. On the morning of August 13, 1961, Berliners awoke to discover that a barbed-wire fence had gone up overnight, separating West and East Berlin and preventing movement between the two sides. The barbed-wire fence was soon expanded to include cement walls and guard towers. The Berlin Wall would stop the flow of people who wanted to flee Communist East Berlin, and it became the most poignant image of the Cold War in Europe. Kennedy's administration quickly condemned the wall, which divided families and limited freedom of movement, but he did not take any action to back up its rhetoric. Khrushchev considered it a soft response and was left with the impression that Kennedy lacked the courage to stand up to a serious challenge.

The Vienna summit was perhaps the worst day of John F. Kennedy's life. As described by Frederick Kempe in his book *Berlin 1961*, Kennedy had been unprepared for Khrushchev's brutality, and Kempe quotes Kennedy as saying that because of the Bay of Pigs, Khrushchev "thought that anyone who was so young and inexperienced as to get into that mess could be taken"; Khrushchev "savaged me" and "beat the hell out of me. . . . I've got a real problem."

The Bay of Pigs and Vienna disasters taught President Kennedy some crucial lessons about leadership and communication. He became almost obsessed with demonstrating strength in words and deeds because he realized that the mere perception of weakness could tempt potential aggressors to test the US resolve, threaten US allies, and destabilize the international order.

———

KENNEDY'S LESSON FOR our generation is simple and powerful: The United States must clearly communicate its will to lead to the rest of the world. Adversaries and allies alike base their decision making in part on their expectations about American behavior on the international scene. If the United States signals weakness, adversaries are emboldened to engage in aggressive and reckless behavior, risking dangerous escalation of otherwise controllable security situations. American signals of weakness also have a contagious effect on American allies, undermining their will to oppose aggressors and support the United States.

Tragically, one of Kennedy's best speeches was never delivered. On November 22, 1963, he was scheduled to give an address to the Dallas Citizens Council, but he never reached his destination. In the planned speech, he stressed the need to back words with strength and action:

> The United States is a peaceful nation. And where our strength and determination are clear, our words need merely to convey conviction, not belligerence. If we are strong, our strength will speak for itself. If we are weak, words will be of no help.

And he concluded:

> We in this country, in this generation are, by destiny rather than choice, the watchmen on the walls of world freedom.

The president was assassinated shortly before he could deliver the speech, but the lines above serve as a powerful summary of Kennedy's legacy and America's special role in world history. John F. Kennedy was exemplary when it came to communicating American resolve to the rest of the world. Future American presidents should be fluent in Kennedy's long list of remarkable foreign-policy speeches.

CHAPTER 4

RONALD REAGAN

Firm Conviction and American Exceptionalism

Our mission is to nourish and defend freedom
and democracy, and communicate these ideals
everywhere we can.
—PRESIDENT RONALD REAGAN

O n October 11, 1986, halfway between Moscow and
Washington, DC, the leaders of the world's two
superpowers met at the stark and picturesque Höfdi
House in Reykjavík, Iceland. Communist Party general secretary Mikhail Gorbachev had proposed the meeting to US
president Ronald Reagan less than thirty days before. Expectations for the Reykjavík summit were low.

Höfdi was originally the house of the French consul in Iceland, and it bears to this day many signs of its original purpose,
such as the letters RF (the abbreviation for *République Française*,
the French Republic), in its architecture. It has welcomed many
famous guests over the years, including the queen of England,
Winston Churchill, and Marlene Dietrich. It has even had, so
the story goes, a supernatural visitor: a ghostly "White Lady." Her
presence once concerned a previous British ambassador so much
that he convinced the British Foreign Office to sell the house.

On October 11 and 12, 1986, the spirit in the house was not supernatural, but, against all expectations, it turned out to be supercharged. Reagan and Gorbachev took their talks forward at a breathtaking pace, breaking entirely new ground and putting the relationship between the superpowers on an unprecedented footing. Gorbachev agreed that human-rights issues were a legitimate topic of discussion, something no previous Soviet leader had ever conceded. A proposal to eliminate all new strategic missiles grew into a discussion, for the first time in history, of the real possibility of eliminating nuclear weapons forever. Aides to both leaders were astonished by the pace of the discussions. A summit that had begun with low expectations had blossomed into one of the most dramatic and potentially productive summits of all time. At one point Reagan even joked with Gorbachev about how to celebrate the dismantling of the last remaining nuclear warhead. In his biography of the president, *Reagan: The Life*, H. W. Brands reports Reagan's jocular words:

> I can imagine us both in ten years getting together again in Iceland to destroy the last Soviet and American missiles under triumphant circumstances. By then I'll be so old that you won't even recognize me. And you will ask in surprise, "Hey Ron, is that really you? What are you doing here?" And we'll have a big celebration over it.

Such language at a summit would be surprising between leaders who are on the same side and share the same values. The fact that it was possible for Reagan to say it, and Gorbachev to accept it in the spirit in which it was meant, at a meeting of the world's two superpowers at a time when a state of cold war existed between them, is nothing less than miraculous.

The 1986 Reykjavík meeting was the most remarkable summit ever held between US and Soviet leaders. In retrospect, it is a tale of two visionary leaders who had the courage to discuss the idealistic dream of a world free of nuclear weapons, and they had the will to try to turn the dream into reality. While they did not reach final agreement on that most sweeping of visions, they achieved an enormous breakthrough that paved the way for the subsequent adoption of two important agreements to reduce the arsenal of nuclear weapons: first, the Intermediate-Range Nuclear Forces Treaty (INF), for the first time eliminating an entire class of nuclear weapons, and second, the Strategic Arms Reduction Treaty (START), which led to a significant removal of strategic nuclear weapons.

Reagan's outstanding achievements in nuclear disarmament go against the left-wing critics of his presidency. He is routinely accused of being a bellicose Cold War warrior, yet he is the president who not only brought the Cold War to an end peacefully, but did so in a manner that allowed freedom and democracy to prevail. The secret behind his success was the unique combination of his firm conviction and his ability to transform that into an effective execution of policies. It was his gift to be able to shape an overwhelming political coalition at home and translate it into determined action abroad. His sincerity was his strength, both in politics and in diplomacy, and it took him to heights that few presidents have ever matched.

———

THE TWIN STRANDS of passionate conviction and decisive action were woven together throughout Reagan's life. Like Truman, he grew up in the Midwest, in Dixon, Illinois. He followed a unique path to the White House. After successful careers as a radio sports announcer, Hollywood movie actor, and television host, he turned to politics relatively late in life. Indeed, his political path itself was far from orthodox. His political outlook was shaped by his parents, both Democrats, and he remained a Democrat until after he turned fifty. In Hollywood in the late 1930s and early 1940s, Reagan identified with Roosevelt's internationalism, especially his opposition to the aggression of Nazi Germany and imperial Japan. After World War II, Reagan aligned with the dominant faction in the Democratic Party: the anti-Communist liberals whose ranks included President Harry Truman and former first lady Eleanor Roosevelt.

Reagan's experience of leadership began long before his formal political career. He joined the Screen Actors Guild (SAG) in 1937, became a member of the union's board in 1941 and its president in 1947, and continued to serve on the board after stepping down from the presidency in 1954. Thus, for more than a decade he was involved in the unique world of Hollywood union management.

It was a time of passionate conflict within SAG, reflecting the wider ideological conflict that dominated the world during the last years of Stalin and the first years of Khrushchev. A number of SAG members were Communist sympathizers; some were Communists themselves. Reagan passionately opposed Communism, and so saw their influence as a threat to everything he believed in. At a meeting in which many Communist sympathizers were present, Reagan stated that Communism was no better than Fascism. As a result, he became the target of attacks and harassment. He experienced firsthand the Communists' boundless intolerance and their authoritarian urge to suppress dissent. He found it shocking that Communism had infiltrated Hollywood and the actors' union so deeply, especially at a time when Soviet spy activity and infiltration were extensive. He took the radical step of cooperating with the Federal Bureau of Investigation, ostensibly to eliminate Communist spies and subversive elements.

The decision remains one of his most controversial, and its justification is challenged to this day. For the student of Reagan's subsequent presidency, however, it is extraordinarily revealing. It shows the strength of his conviction that Communism must be opposed, no matter what the cost, and it shows his determination to go beyond rhetoric in order to use all available instruments of power in fighting it. Those two principles were the foundation of his Soviet policy.

Reagan's politics changed in the 1950s, partly influenced by his new job at General Electric. GE wanted to sponsor a television show, *The General Electric Theater*, with Reagan as host. Reagan took the job, and as part of it, he made many visits to General Electric plants and facilities. There he met workers as well as middle and senior managers, and listened to stories from real life about how red tape and high taxes made life hard and hampered the initiative of businesses and their employees. He developed a strong belief in the power of the free-market economy, protection of private property, and limited government.

Impelled by that belief, he came to identify more and more with Republicans, and in 1962, his fifty-first year, he became a registered Republican.

It was as a Republican that he was elected governor of California in 1966, serving eight years. It was as a Republican that he twice ran unsuccessfully for president, in 1968 and 1976. And it was as a Republican that, in 1980, during a time of US economic troubles and foreign-policy difficulties, he won his party's presidential nomination and defeated President Jimmy Carter to become the fortieth president of the United States.

When Reagan took office, public confidence in government was at its lowest ebb since the Great Depression. A passionate believer in the American way and the American people, his greatest goal was to make Americans believe in themselves again, and the fact that he achieved it may rank as his greatest single achievement. In return, that renewed American self-belief translated into belief in the president: In 1984, Reagan was re-elected in a forty-nine-state landslide. During the eight years of his presidency, he reshaped national politics and carried out his campaign promises to cut taxes and increase the defense budget, using the latter as leverage to negotiate significant arms-control agreements with the Soviet Union. Despite some setbacks, including notable budget deficits, Reagan left office in 1989 with strong approval ratings. He was a giant among American presidents, and that is how he is still remembered.

Reagan won two of the most convincing election victories in American history in large part because he spoke to American voters in terms that were both familiar and inspiring to them. The strong mandate that these elections gave him also strengthened his hand on the international scene. Domestically, Reagan was able to push through large increases in defense spending, which is always a challenge in democratic nations where voters naturally prefer tax cuts and domestically oriented spending. Internationally, Reagan's landslide victories sent a powerful signal to the Soviet Union and other adversaries, as well as allies, that Reagan had political room for maneuver.

———

FOR AMERICANS, AND for Reagan himself, his greatest achievement was his ability to reignite their self-belief. For the rest of the world, however, he has gone down in history as the man who did more than any other to bring the Cold War to a close without firing a shot. Both successes were based on a single principle, one that guided him throughout his career: Strong, effective policies are best based on strong convictions.

Informed by his experiences in SAG and his own perception of the Stalinist regime, Reagan regarded Communism as an immoral and destructive ideology and believed that the Soviet Union was bent on world domination. In a famous speech he delivered on March 8, 1983, he called the Soviets "the focus of evil in the modern world" and referred to the Soviet Union as an "evil empire." He never doubted the supremacy of free societies. In a speech to the British House of Commons on June 8, 1982, he declared that "freedom and democracy will leave Marxism and Leninism on the ash heap of history." On June 12, 1987, Reagan visited West Berlin, and, like President Kennedy before him, he delivered a memorable speech. Referring to the wall that divided West and East Berlin, he declared: "This wall will fall. For it cannot withstand faith; it cannot withstand truth. The wall cannot withstand freedom." And addressing directly the Soviet leader, Mr. Gorbachev, President Reagan proclaimed: "Mr. Gorbachev, open this gate. Mr. Gorbachev, tear down this wall!"

That speech has gone down in history: the most memorable public appeal ever made by an American leader to a Soviet one, and one that, in just a few short years, would see its fulfillment. Would Reagan have been able to make that speech if he had not struck up such a rapport with Gorbachev in Reykjavík the year before? We will never know, but the consciousness of knowing his opponent must surely have reinforced his conviction that the Berlin Wall, and Communism itself, must both fall.

But just as in Hollywood in the 1950s, Reagan was determined to turn his conviction into action. Rhetoric was not enough. He believed that it was necessary for the United States to combat the spread of Soviet-backed Marxist and leftist regimes throughout the world. In his State of the Union address on February 6, 1985, he established what came to be known as the Reagan Doctrine: The United States should support anti-Communist insurgents wherever they might be. He proclaimed:

> We must stand by all our democratic allies. And we must not break faith with those who are risking their lives—on every continent, from Afghanistan to Nicaragua—to defy Soviet-supported aggression and secure rights which have been ours from birth. . . . Support for freedom fighters is self-defense.

Reagan reaffirmed his strong belief in the power of freedom and democracy, and formulated a wide-ranging strategy of American global leadership in protecting and promoting liberty:

Freedom is not the sole prerogative of a chosen few; it is the universal right of all God's children. Look to where peace and prosperity flourish today. It is in the homes that freedom built. Victories against poverty are greatest and peace most secure where people live by laws that ensure free press, free speech, and freedom to worship, vote and create wealth. Our mission is to nourish and defend freedom and democracy, and to communicate these ideals everywhere we can. America's economic success is freedom's success; it can be repeated a hundred times in a hundred different nations.

In action, the Reagan Doctrine translated into covertly supporting the contras in their fight against the leftist Sandinista government in Nicaragua; the Afghan rebels in their fight against the Soviet occupiers; and anti-Communist Angolan forces involved in that nation's civil war. American support for these "freedom fighters" was not without controversy, and not all its consequences were positive, but in his farewell address in 1989, Reagan claimed success in weakening the Sandinista government, forcing the Soviets to withdraw from Afghanistan, and bringing an end to the conflict in Angola. Above all, Reagan could rejoice in an emerging thaw in relations between the United States and the Soviet Union, due not least to his firm stance in pushing back against the expansionism of international Communism. The Soviets eventually realized that the Communist system simply was not able to cope with freedom, capitalism, and resolute American global leadership.

———

BUT IT WOULD be a mistake to believe that Reagan's foreign policy was based on anti-Communism alone. First and foremost, it was founded on a powerful conviction of the economic and moral superiority of capitalism and democracy. Reagan firmly believed that political freedom and a free-market economy were the free world's unbeatable weapons in its battle against totalitarianism. In Reagan's eyes, the Cold War was the struggle between might and right: a clash between the principle that the state should control its citizens and the principle that the citizens should control the state.

Reagan never doubted the ability of democratic societies to outcompete the Soviet Union politically, economically, and militarily. He firmly believed that America's obvious power and prosperity were the best argument for political and economic freedom. And in an inspired stroke of intuition, he reasoned that the more obvious he could make the argument, the stronger the argument would be. In one of his favorite stories, he would describe how the landscape looked from his helicopter as he flew to the presidential retreat at Camp David—full of houses with little backyard swimming pools and automobiles in the driveways. "I have a fantasy about having Mr. Gorbachev beside me," the president once said, "and being able to point down and say, 'Those are the homes of American workers and they own them!'"

As president, Reagan promoted economic policies aimed at stimulating economic growth and free enterprise. The four pillars of his economic policy were to lower taxes, reduce regulation, restrain government spending, and reduce inflation through a noninflationary monetary policy. At the beginning of his presidency he cut taxes drastically, by 25 percent, including reducing the top marginal tax rate from 70 percent to less than 30 percent. The philosophy behind the tax cuts was that lower taxes would actually increase government revenue because it would provide a greater incentive to work, produce, and invest, and a greater capacity to consume. Critics called it, scornfully, "voodoo economics."

Having trained as an economist, I was one of many commentators who viewed Reagan's politics with initial skepticism. I had been taught John Maynard Keynes's theories of demand-side economics. Demand-siders believed that unemployment could be reduced and economic activity could be increased through government action aimed at boosting demand for goods and services, for example, through higher public spending. However, as a young member of the Danish parliament, I visited the University of Chicago in the summer of 1982, and that visit was an eye-opener. The Chicago school of economics is a famous free-market-oriented economic philosophy, and my meeting with members of the faculty had an enormous impact on my career. Some people have spiritual or religious awakenings, but for me this was an economic awakening, and I started challenging the economic theories I had been taught at school at home.

In Chicago, I was introduced to supply-side economics. In essence, the supply-siders argue that government can stimulate the economy more effectively through indirect action, by cutting taxes and red tape in order to increase the incentive to work. In other words, where demand-siders believe that governments can get more by intervening more, supply-siders believe that governments can get more by intervening less. I learned about the Laffer curve—a theoretical graph showing that reducing tax rates could increase tax revenues by stimulating economic activity. As a classical European liberal, believing in free markets and the power of the individual, I was receptive to that message. Having met with numerous people from all walks of life during my American educational journey and listened to their reports about the nascent economic optimism, I left the United States fully convinced that Reaganomics would work. And the fact is that the US economy started to grow after years of stagnation, millions of new jobs were created, and family incomes grew significantly. When Reagan left office, unemployment, inflation, and interest rates were lower than when he took office. While the public deficit grew due to massive military spending, America's economic progress was widely recognized and sent a powerful signal of American vigor to friends and foes alike.

Reagan transformed that economic muscle into military and foreign-policy strength.

———

FROM THE BEGINNING of his presidency, Reagan took a number of steps to enhance American military power, to counter Communist expansionism, and to communicate in clear language his opposition to Communism and the Soviet Union's suppression of its neighboring nations. Reagan vowed to rebuild the American military after the Vietnam debacle and the years of stagnation that followed, and to confront the Soviet Union and its allies with new vigor and purpose. He was convinced that, if America put all its efforts into converting economic potential into military strength, the Soviets would be unable to compete and would come to the bargaining table.

Reagan was of the firm belief that the Soviet Union was a colossus with feet of clay. Unlike many others, including some of his advisers, he believed that the Soviet Union could be overcome by the use of economic tools. The key would be to make the United States so economically and militarily strong that the Soviet Union could not afford to catch up with the leader of the free world. This would lead to the Soviet Union's collapse. Thus, Reagan gave military spending priority over his promise of a balanced budget. The defense budget in his first term more than doubled. These funds were allocated to a wide array of new weapons systems, research and development, and improvements in combat readiness and troop mobility.

In March 1983, Reagan unveiled his plan for a missile-defense system called the Strategic Defense Initiative (SDI), which critics derided as "Star Wars," after the name of the popular movie series. The purpose of this system was to protect the American people from attack by long-range—and potentially nuclear-armed—missiles; in other words, to make nuclear weapons obsolete by making attacks impossible because the missiles would be destroyed before they reached their targets. It was an ambitious project, and it made the Soviet leadership deeply concerned, because it would have gravely undermined the Soviet Union's nuclear strength, and the Soviet Union would not be able to compete with the United States in this arms race—either economically or technologically. That is why Gorbachev made the abandonment of SDI a central point of his demands in Reykjavík. However, Reagan refused to give any concessions in that regard, and in retrospect, his refusal to budge was the main reason why the summit ended inconclusively.

Reagan was convinced that the Soviet Union had not abided by treaty obligations to maintain nuclear parity among the superpowers. The Soviets were rapidly deploying intermediate-range nuclear missiles in Eastern Europe, the SS-20 missiles. The United States' allies in Western Europe felt threatened by this aggressive nuclear buildup within the Warsaw Pact. This development prompted the NATO Double-Track Decision. On the diplomatic track, the Soviet Union would be called on to halt the deployment of nuclear missiles in Eastern Europe, while NATO and the Warsaw Pact should agree on a mutual reduction and limitation of nuclear missiles. If that track failed to bear fruit, NATO (i.e., the United States) would deploy more nuclear weapons in Western Europe. In Europe, the Double-Track approach provoked a lot of opposition from left-wing groups, very often inspired by Soviet propaganda. But thanks to President Reagan and his determined leadership, Europe's political leaders stood their ground, the Double-Track Decision was unanimously approved by NATO members, and an unmistakable signal of Western unity and decisiveness was sent to the Kremlin. Eventually, the Soviet leaders realized that the Soviet Union could not afford this nuclear buildup, and in 1987 Reagan and Gorbachev agreed to destroy all middle-range missiles through the INF Treaty, an indirect product of the Reykjavík summit one year earlier.

Reagan was proven right: The decisive American military buildup encouraged the Soviets to come to the bargaining table and facilitated political dialogue and arms reductions. But beyond that, the buildup showed America's traditional allies that he meant business and was sincere in the defense of their interests. Thanks to what some might consider hawkish policies, Reagan gained the leverage to engage the Soviet leader in a political and diplomatic process. Once again it was demonstrated that strong diplomacy works best when it is built on the foundation of strong military forces and a strong will.

Reagan was a consummate diplomat, a man who knew how to give and take, but who also knew when to stand firm in defense of principles that he believed sacrosanct. In the conflict with Communism that defined his presidency to the outside world, Reagan believed strongly in the power of freedom, and he had no doubts about the attractiveness of the Western ideals. He rejected the self-doubt that had infected the American approach to foreign policy after the Vietnam War and emphasized vigorously the power of Western ideals to win the battle for hearts and minds in the world. For him, the Cold War was basically a battle of values—between an autocratic and oppressive Communist system inspired and led by the Soviet Union and a democratic and liberal capitalist system inspired and led by the United States.

In this battle, Reagan firmly believed that the United States could only deal with an expansionist and aggressive state like the Soviet Union through superior power and a firm stance. This conviction was, to a large degree, founded on "the lesson of Munich," the failure of appeasement prior to World War II. But Reagan was also of the firm belief that it was a built-in characteristic of the Soviet system to bend only when it was confronted with an overwhelming power. All attempts to meet "legitimate" Soviet concerns would be counterproductive. Rather than promoting dialogue and rapprochement, these attempts would be perceived as Western weakness, encourage the Soviet Union to continued intransigence, and strengthen the Soviet belief in Communist invincibility.

It was Reagan's steadfast belief that only overwhelming power and the willingness to use it would deter the Soviet Union from continued expansionism, and he was convinced that the strength of the American and Western societies would eventually force the Soviets to the negotiating table. The most efficient way to engage in a constructive dialogue with the Soviet Union was to negotiate from a position of strength. He had formulated that position as far back as 1976 during his unsuccessful bid for the presidency. In his campaign address on March 31, 1976, he stated, "Peace does not come from weakness or retreat. It comes from the restoration of American military superiority." During his presidency, the formula became "peace through strength," and Reagan's focus on negotiating from a position of strength proved right.

———

REAGAN'S DEMOCRAT POLITICS throughout the first half-century of his life could have weakened him in the eyes of both the party he left and the party he joined; part of his genius was his ability to turn it into a strength. Due to his understanding of the experiences and emotions of both parties, he was able to build a strong and unconventional domestic coalition that gave him considerable room to maneuver to cut taxes, increase defense spending, and exert a firm policy toward the Soviet Union. The great popular support for Reagan was based on a coalition of traditional Republicans and the so-called Reagan Democrats, socially conservative Democrats who were attracted by Reagan's robust foreign policy.

Furthermore, Reagan managed to transform that popular support into a forceful coalition in Congress. Indeed, during his first term as president, Reagan had to deal with a Democratic-controlled House, while the Senate was held by the Republicans. But he demonstrated great skills as a coalition builder, inviting swing congressmen to talks in the White House and at Camp David. It also helped that he had well-developed ties and an excellent personal relationship with the Democratic leadership, notably the House Speaker, Tip O'Neill. But first and foremost, he used his special talent as a popular communicator. When Reagan had a major project that had been met with opposition in Congress, he appealed directly to the American people through carefully crafted TV appearances. His appeals had a powerful effect: After them, members of Congress were flooded with letters and phone calls from constituents who wanted their congressman to support the president. No president since Kennedy had shown such an ability to use the media to mobilize support for his policies. This made it possible for Reagan to reach out directly to the public at large and put a maximum of pressure on his opponents in Congress.

But most important, Reagan was able to harvest his political victories because he so effectively encapsulated the core American values and instilled new optimism in American society. "It's morning again in America" became the catchphrase for his American economic and political revival, and was used in the Reagan campaign for reelection in 1984 in television ads that reinforced the message by saying, "Under the leadership of President Reagan, our country is prouder, and stronger and better." That sent an unmistakable message of strength and resolve and optimism to the American people, as well as friends and adversaries abroad.

———

ANY LEADER MUST emanate a firm conviction and self-confidence to get people to follow. For the United States, the will to lead entails a firm belief in the exceptional position of America as the world's predominant power; an acceptance of the country's exceptional strength, obligation, and responsibility; and self-confidence in the basic principles of freedom upon which America has been built. Furthermore, global leadership is only sustainable with a strong domestic political mandate. For America to truly have the will to lead, the American president must be backed by a strong political coalition; otherwise, America's foreign policy constantly risks being undercut by America's political games.

Ronald Reagan is a great example of an American president who exuded conviction and confidence and was able to mobilize a strong political coalition. When he took office, the United States was struggling with the cultural and political fallout from Vietnam and the economic crisis of the 1970s. When he left office, the Communist bloc was on the verge of worldwide collapse and the United States was in the midst of a boom of economic growth and innovation. Reagan's belief in American exceptionalism was never in doubt. Again and again he alluded to a special purpose for America, as in his Thanksgiving message in 1982:

> I have always believed that this anointed land was set apart in an uncommon way; that a divine plan placed this great continent here between the oceans to be found by people from every corner of the Earth who had a special love of faith and freedom.

Not surprisingly, one of Reagan's favorite metaphors for America was the "city upon a hill," a term taken from John Winthrop's sermon "A Model of Christian Charity" from 1630. In his farewell address on January 11, 1989, Reagan referred to Winthrop as "an early pilgrim, an early freedom man," and ended with an emotional and powerful vision for America.

I have spoken of the shining city all my political life but I don't know if I ever quite communicated what I saw when I said it. But in my mind it was a tall proud city built on rocks stronger than oceans, windswept, God-blessed, and teeming with people of all kinds living in harmony and peace. A city with free ports that hummed with commerce and creativity, and if there had to be city walls, the walls had doors and the doors were open to anyone with the will and the heart to get here. That's how I saw it and see it still.

"A city upon a hill" is a phrase from the parable of salt and light in Jesus's Sermon on the Mount. In Matthew 5:14, he tells his listeners, "You are the light of the world: a city that is set on a hill cannot be hidden." Still aboard the ship *Arbella*, the Puritan Winthrop admonished the future Massachusetts Bay colonists that their future would be "as a city upon a hill," watched by the world, which became the idea on which New England colonists based their hilly capital city, Boston.

Reagan was not the only president to speak metaphorically about the "city upon a hill." So did President Kennedy. On

January 9, 1961, Kennedy turned the phrase to prominence during an address delivered to the General Court of Massachusetts:

> I have been guided by the standard John Winthrop set before his shipmates on the flagship *Arbella* 331 years ago, as they, too, faced the task of building a new government on a perilous frontier. "We must always consider," he said, "that we shall be as a city upon a hill—the eyes of all people are upon us." Today the eyes of all people are truly upon us—and our governments, in every branch, at every level, national, state and local, must be as a city upon a hill—constructed and inhabited by men aware of their great trust and their great responsibilities.

At their core, both Kennedy and Reagan believed that America is exceptional, as they believed that there was something special about America that sets the nation apart from the other nations of the world. Reagan continually made deliberate attempts to help Americans rediscover the greatness of the nation by sharing what he believed made America an exceptional and great nation. Based on this firm conviction, he exercised determined American global leadership that eventually brought the Soviet Union and international Communism to a collapse and ended the Cold War.

———

IN RECENT YEARS, it has become politically incorrect in some circles to speak of "American exceptionalism." This is unfortunate, for without a firm belief in America's special role in the world, the American electorate is unlikely to support the burden of American global leadership. It is no coincidence that Russian president Vladimir Putin chose the term "American exceptionalism" as his theme in a *New York Times* op-ed article in September 2013. Putin's article was published as a response to President Obama's reference to American exceptionalism during his speech on Syria a few days earlier. Putin wrote:

> It is extremely dangerous to encourage people to see them-selves as exceptional, whatever the motivation. There are big countries and small countries, rich and poor, those with long democratic traditions and those still finding their way to democracy. Their policies differ too. We are all different, but when we ask for the Lord's blessing, we must not forget that God created us equal.

The latter was, of course, a polemical reference to the lan-guage of the Declaration of Independence from 1776.

Obviously, you should always be careful in using the term "exceptional," in particular if it represents a moral judgment that "you are better than others." To my mind, the term "American exceptionalism" rather reflects the fact that the United States is different from other countries in a very special way. It is an undeniable fact that America occupies an exceptional position in the world, whether Mr. Putin likes it or not.

First of all, America holds a unique geographical location. Besides Mexico and Canada, the United States is the only major country to have direct access to both the Pacific and Atlantic Oceans. This unique geography offers logistical and military advantages. Whereas other big powers—for instance, China,

Russia, and India—have common, tense borders to defend, forcing them to devote a lot of resources and attention to local and regional issues, America is free from such regional challenges and can focus on executing a global leadership role. On top of that, the United States possesses vast natural resources, including some of the world's most productive agricultural land and largest energy reserves. In recent years, advanced hydraulic fracturing technology has added yet another dimension to the American economic potential. Soon the United States will be self-sufficient when it comes to energy, which will drastically change the geopolitical landscape and add further to American power.

Next, the development of the United States as a nation is exceptional. The United States has been a melting pot. For centuries it has attracted people from all over the world who long for freedom and opportunity. The United States re-creates itself by attracting the best and brightest from the rest of the world and blending them into a diverse culture of creativity. That gives a formidable strength to the American economy, but it also expands America's ties with peoples and cultures all over the world.

Finally, the idealism upon which the United States is founded and the development of mature, solid democratic institutions are truly exceptional. The early American colonists came from Europe very much inspired by the European Enlightenment. The Enlightenment was crucial in determining almost every aspect of colonial America— most notably in terms of politics, government, and religion. Concepts such as freedom from oppression, free speech, natural rights, and new ways of thinking about government structure came straight from Enlightenment philosophers. Montesquieu's idea about the balance of power among the three branches of government was explicitly used, just as Rousseau's ideas about the power of democracy and consent of the people were used in the formation of government.

This history of American democracy has added other enduring advantages to American strength. The American foundation on the idea of individual rights and personal liberty has a universal attraction—maybe not in the circles of autocratic elites that rule some nations under kleptocracy and oppression, but certainly among ordinary people who look to America as the inspiring flame of freedom, "the shining city on the hill" that they would very much like to live in. Being the world's oldest democracy, the United States has succeeded in developing strong, mature democratic institutions, tested and tried over time. And while democratic evolution is perpetual, undoubtedly the American governmental structures are the strongest in the world, and clearly fit for global leadership.

My point here is not to state the obvious, but to highlight that these evident facts have broader implications than immediately meet the eye. A position of fundamental strength necessarily impacts the way that other powers view America, and therefore imposes a leadership role on the United States whether Americans choose to accept it or not. The question is not what America's role in the world should be, but whether America chooses to play this role with the gusto and conviction that a star performance requires.

––––––

PRESIDENTS TRUMAN, Kennedy, and Reagan were all star performers in their own way. Despite their differences— different personalities, different family backgrounds, different upbringings, and different life experiences—they were none-theless united in their view of American exceptionalism and in the conviction that America has a special role in the world and a special responsibility to exercise global leadership in defense of freedom and democracy.

Each had his own strengths. President Truman was effective in conducting a policy that established strong institutions as the framework for a new international order. He rebuilt the house of the nations after the devastation of two world wars. President Kennedy was an outstanding communicator, who was an inspiring beacon for the entire free world during the most threatening period of the Cold War. He held the torch of freedom high and lit the world with it. While President Reagan was also a great speaker, his strength was primarily his staunch belief in the superiority of capitalism and the inferiority of Communism. He turned back the tide of Soviet imperialism and made the Iron Curtain shake.

While Truman's and Kennedy's policies toward the Soviet Union and international Communism were based on the assumption that the Soviet Union was an economically, technologically, and militarily strong power, Reagan had the clear view that Soviet Communism was basically weak and could be defeated by means of economic warfare, backed by strong and credible military deterrence.

Consequently, Truman and Kennedy pursued an essentially defensive containment policy toward the Soviet Union, while Reagan pursued an offensive policy by countering international Communist expansionism. First and foremost, Reagan wanted to force the Soviet Union to its knees economically by developing an unbeatably strong US economy and demonstrating to the world's Communist nations that capitalism is the most efficient system to meet people's basic needs. To paraphrase Kennedy, President Reagan mobilized American capitalism and sent it into battle.

All three had the courage to break with the isolationism that had surrounded them in their early years, and to mark themselves as their own men, free of the limitations of their pasts. Truman spoke out early in favor of American internationalism, thus pursuing a policy that ran counter to the Missouri voters' conventional inclination toward isolationism. Kennedy distanced himself from his father's pronounced isolationism; and Reagan not only switched from the Democrats to the Republicans, he also eliminated the current of isolationism, or rather noninterference, that had characterized parts of the Republican Party since President Herbert Hoover.

In his book *Profiles in Courage*, about the bravery and integrity of eight US senators who had the courage to defy the opinion of their party and constituents to do what they felt was right, then–Senator Kennedy wrote: "This is a book about that most admirable of human virtues—courage." Aiming at the threatening Soviet Communist dictatorship, he continued:

> Only the very courageous will be able to take the hard and unpopular decisions necessary for our survival in the struggle with a powerful enemy—an enemy with leaders who need give little thought to the popularity of their course. . . . And only the very courageous will be able to keep alive the spirit of individualism and dissent which gave birth to this nation.

Presidents Truman, Kennedy, and Reagan had the courage. Holding office at the beginning of the Cold War, the crisis itself, and the end of the Cold War, respectively, they had the moral and political bravery to make the hard and unpopular decisions, for the sake of freedom and democracy. They fought the forces of totalitarianism abroad, without using its methods at home. They are shining and exemplary illustrations of how American global leadership can be performed efficiently. Of course, they made mistakes, and they suffered their defeats. But overall, their presidencies were a success, and they showed that determined American leadership can protect and promote freedom and democracy, ensure peace, and keep autocracy and oppression at bay.

CHAPTER 5

AMERICA AS GLOBAL POLICEMAN
The Case for Intervention

Life so long untroubled, that ye who inherit forget
It was not made with the mountains; it is not one with the deep.
Men, not gods, devised it. Men, not gods, must keep.
—RUDYARD KIPLING, *The Islanders*

On May 8, 2003, I had a very early breakfast with President Bush at the White House. We had had problems finding time for a meeting, but we both thought it was of utmost importance to meet. In March, the American-led international coalition had occupied Iraq. Denmark supported this mission, and after the initial successful military operation we had to prepare for the restoration of Iraqi society. There was a lot to discuss, but our schedulers gave up trying to squeeze in a meeting. However, the president was an early bird, so he personally intervened and suggested a breakfast meeting at 7:10 a.m, during which we could go for a run together. I am an early starter and a keen runner as well, and we had already agreed to go running together on an official visit he had planned to Denmark, so I willingly accepted.

My entry into the White House that morning was memorable. The security procedures were at a minimum; I guess they reasoned that only a very trustworthy person would meet the president that early in the morning. The cleaning was still going on, so, watched by astonished cleaners, I fought my way over vacuum cleaners, wires, and hoses and ended up in a very small room. The breakfast took place in the president's private dining room in the West Wing, behind the Oval Office. The room is so small that there is space for only four people at the table.

Only two people were there: President Bush and his national security adviser, Condoleezza Rice. I was accompanied by the Danish ambassador to the United States, Ulrik Federspiel. After a warm welcome we got seated, and the president asked what we would like for breakfast. The selection was vast: seasonal fruit, muffins, scrambled eggs, bacon and sausage, orange juice, water, and coffee. Before we could answer, the president himself said, "Actually, I would like cornflakes," and he asked a waiter to go and pick up a selection of cornflakes from his private kitchen.

In the meantime, the president expressed regrets that we had to cancel our run, but in fact he couldn't go jogging any longer because of a torn ligament. Not only that, he doubted that he would be able to resume jogging. "I'm sorry to hear that," I said, and added, "I had charted a three-mile track at home and trained for our planned run."

Now the waiter returned with three different boxes of cornflakes. We agreed to try all of them, and the president himself readily served the cereals, accompanied by recommendations of the different kinds.

In this intimate setting we had an extremely open and frank discussion about the international situation. Typically for Bush, he used that occasion to inquire about my assessment of European politics and European political leaders. He was furious with President Jacques Chirac of France and Chancellor Gerhard Schröder of Germany, who had split Europe and the transatlantic alliance. He felt betrayed by Schröder, who had "lied in the Oval Office," and Chirac was simply anti-American: He had "bullied the Eastern Europeans" and tried to undermine the British prime minister, Tony Blair. Though President Putin of Russia had joined Chirac and Schröder in a coalition against the Iraq War, George Bush was much more forgiving in his assessment of the Russian president. Putin had "miscalculated"—he was still up against domestic bureaucracy, corruption, and an old-fashioned military establishment. But the United States had a "strategic deal" with Russia, and the United States would help Russia.

It was enormously valuable to be able to talk together openly, to discuss our perceptions of the global situation and our plans for how to react to it. But for me, the main value of the meeting was that it confirmed to me President Bush's determination, and his country's ability, to act as the world's policeman.

The need for a policeman was there in 1990, when Saddam Hussein invaded Kuwait; it was there a decade later, when he flouted the demands of the international community over his weapons program; it is still there today. The bleak truth is that there are regimes in the world that would like nothing better than to be able to break the rules of the international community and get away with it, and they will only stick with the rules if they know that transgressions will be punished. The world needs a policeman to make sure that the international rules that shaped our world—and our prosperity—are honored. And the only country with the strength and credibility to carry out that task is the United States.

The Policeman and the Gatekeeper

As we have already seen, the United States occupies a unique, and uniquely privileged, geographic position in the world. When it comes to the global village, the United States is a big, rich house with a wall and a moat around it. As well as being a privilege, this position is also a temptation, because uniquely among the world's leading powers, the United States can always choose not to get involved in foreign conflicts. Europe has all the troubles of North Africa, the Middle East, and Russia on its doorstep; China has neighbors North Korea and the South China Sea; Russia, as well as picking unnecessary and illegal fights with its neighbors, has to deal with the instability of Central Asia and the North Caucasus. These countries all live in more or less dangerous neighborhoods; the United States does not.

Throughout history, that privileged position has allowed America to swing between two opposing roles. At times, the United States has acted as the world's policeman, the one that keeps order in the village and makes sure everyone else sticks to the rules. At other times, it has preferred to be its own gatekeeper, ignoring what was going on in the street outside unless it impacted directly on American security.

Ever since the Cold War, the pendulum has swung back and forth between the policeman and the gatekeeper, between advocates of early intervention (policeman) and isolation (gatekeeper). Right now, it is the gatekeeper instinct that dominates, but it is my firm belief that the next president will have to push the pendulum back the other way because the world is more secure, and the United States is safer, when America chooses to be the policeman early on and plays the role with conviction.

This chapter will therefore analyze the way the pendulum has swung back and forth since the end of the Cold War. It will examine the reasons why the pendulum has swung at specific times, and the effects that American action and inaction have had. And it will address the question of why the United States, and no other country, is suited to play the role of the world's policeman.

The 1990s

The early 1990s were an unforgettable time in human history—a time of relief, and of belief. The Cold War had just ended, the threat of nuclear war had been lifted, dictatorships were turning almost overnight into democracies, and there was real hope that the world was about to become a better and more peaceful place.

President George H. W. Bush put that belief into words in his State of the Union address on January 16, 1991: "We have before us the opportunity to forge for ourselves and for future generations a new world order—a world where the rule of law, not the law of the jungle, governs the conduct of nations."

But he was not speaking in abstract terms: He was referring to a very specific conflict. Five months earlier, in August 1990, the Iraqi dictator, Saddam Hussein, had sent a force of one hundred thousand Iraqi troops to invade their small but wealthy neighbor, Kuwait, claiming that it was historically Iraqi territory. The Iraqi troops subjected the people of Kuwait to unspeakable atrocities, systematically raping, pillaging, and plundering a tiny nation that posed no conceivable threat to Iraq.

It was a challenge to the international community, and to the concept of "the rule of law, not the law of the jungle," and President Bush was determined not to let it pass. In his address to the nation, he underlined that his purpose was to protect a world order where "no nation will be permitted to brutally assault its neighbor." He chose, in fact, to be the world's policeman.

In that role, the United States led efforts to organize an international coalition that, working through the UN Security Council, passed United Nations resolutions demanding Iraq's immediate and unconditional withdrawal. After the deadline for withdrawal passed, the coalition attacked Iraq by air. Within twenty-four hours, coalition forces controlled the skies, bombarding such strategic sites as Iraqi command and control facilities, Saddam Hussein's palaces, power stations, intelligence and security facilities, oil refineries, arms factories, and Iraq's missile facilities. Coalition aircraft subsequently targeted Iraqi troops in Kuwait. Comprising troops from thirty-four countries, including a number of Arab states, the coalition forces liberated Kuwait and forced the Iraqi forces to withdraw.

The First Gulf War was unprecedented in the use of high-technology and precision weapons, and losses on the Allied side were limited. Only the United States could have sent over half a million service members thousands of miles to carry out a precise military operation successfully in a matter of weeks; only the United States could have built such a broad international coalition so quickly. Had the United States refrained from taking action, Saddam Hussein would have succeeded in occupying a neighboring country, and this would have set a bad precedent and sent a dangerous message to unscrupulous dictators elsewhere in the world.

But the pendulum quickly swung back under the presidency of Bill Clinton, whose first foreign intervention ended in disaster. In 1993, the American military experienced a catastrophic failure of action in Somalia, where US troops were killed and dragged through the streets of the capital, Mogadishu. It was, at the time, the greatest loss of American soldiers in combat since the Vietnam War, and it appears to have traumatized the White House, especially as the losses occurred in an area that was of no vital interest to the United States. For the next two years, Clinton avoided intervention, preferring to act as the gatekeeper of American security rather than policeman of the world.

But the result was calamitous, both in Africa and in Europe. In Africa, 1994 saw one of the bloodiest events in the history of the continent: the Rwandan genocide. This pitted Hutu extremists in Rwanda's political elite against the Tutsi minority population, whom they blamed for the country's growing economic and social problems. In April 1994, a plane carrying the country's Hutu president was shot down. In reaction, Hutu extremists started a bloodbath with the goal of destroying the entire Tutsi population. It is estimated that perhaps as many as three-quarters of the Tutsi population was slaughtered, and at the same time, thousands of Hutus were assassinated because they opposed the genocide and opposed the extremist groups that carried out the killings. Overall, up to a million people were killed in the Rwandan genocide.

All that while, America did nothing; indeed, according to Samantha Power, author of the Pulitzer Prize–winning book *"A Problem from Hell": America and the Age of Genocide* and now the US ambassador to the UN, the United States was not only passive, refraining from sending troops, but worked aggressively to block the authorization of UN reinforcements. Even as thousands of Rwandans were being butchered every day, US officials shunned the term "genocide" for fear of being obliged to act and, perhaps, risk US troops on the ground again.

Clinton subsequently declared that what he regrets most about his presidency is the lack of action to stop the genocide in Rwanda. In an interview with CNBC in March 2013, he said, "If we'd gone in sooner, I believe we could have saved at least a third of the lives that were lost. . . . It had an enduring impact on me." By that count, hundreds of thousands of deaths could have been averted. The fact that they were not is a stain on Clinton's presidency.

Yet it took another genocide to break the Clinton administration out of the gatekeeper mentality, this time in the Balkans. Here, the years 1991 to 1995 marked the disintegration of Yugoslavia under the pressure of ethnic conflict, economic issues, and the oppression of the government of Slobodan Milošević. The ensuing war lasted over three years. Initially, the Clinton administration considered the situation in the Balkans as a primarily European problem, best addressed by the then newborn European Union (formally created by the Maastricht Treaty in February 1992). However, European governments maintained a wait-and-see attitude. There was little European domestic support for armed intervention, while many Americans were reluctant to commit to a role in the Balkans, fearing a protracted occupation or guerrilla warfare. Over the next three years, the war in Bosnia-Herzegovina claimed around one hundred thousand lives and displaced millions from their homes as Europe witnessed the most horrific fighting on its territory since the end of World War II.

The defining tragedy of the Balkan wars was the Srebrenica genocide, in July 1995. Eight thousand Muslim Bosniaks, mainly men and boys, were killed by Bosnian Serb army units. The UN had declared Srebrenica a safe area under UN protection; however, the Dutch UN soldiers stationed there to maintain the safe area failed to prevent the town's capture by the Serbs and the subsequent massacre. It was the worst crime committed on European soil since the time of Hitler and Stalin.

At last the United States swung into action. This was done through NATO, and through extensive diplomatic efforts, notably through the dispatch of the energetic American diplomat Richard Holbrooke to the region. In August 1995, galvanized into action by the US leadership, NATO executed an intense two-week series of attacks on Bosnian Serb military positions. The combination of NATO's air campaign and Ambassador Holbrooke's tireless diplomacy yielded a cease-fire by the end of September. Two more months of intensive negotiations led to the conclusion of the Dayton Accords, putting an end to the Bosnian war, in November 1995; and in December, the NATO-led Implementation Force (IFOR) deployed into Bosnia to keep the fragile peace.

The Lessons of Genocide

There are a number of lessons to be drawn from the genocides of 1994–95. The first is that it takes enormous time and effort to stir the United Nations into action. In Rwanda, the UN and

Belgium, the former colonial power, had forces on the ground but no mandate to stop the killing. France, an ally of the Hutu government, sent a force to establish a safe zone but was accused of not doing enough to stop the slaughter in the area. The United States, according to Samantha Power, blocked attempts at action. By the time the international community agreed that something needed to be done, it was far too late.

The second lesson is that, even when the UN is involved, it is only as strong as its mandate. In the Balkans, that mandate was simply not strong enough. I well remember an incident in April 1994, when a Danish peacekeeping contingent got fed up with the UN's passivity. A UN observation post had come under heavy artillery fire from the Serbs. While trying to relieve the observation post, a Danish tank squadron was ambushed and attacked with antitank missiles. The Danes requested air support, but almost unbelievably under the circumstances, their request was rejected. The Danish commander, Colonel Lars R. Moeller, then decided to act on his own initiative, returned fire, and destroyed several Serbian artillery pieces, an ammunition dump, and several bunkers. The Serb attacks ceased after this Danish counterattack. The Danish commander subsequently named the encounter Operation Hooligan Bashing. This incident was remarkable because it was one of the largest engagements that took place between the UN forces and the military units involved in the war in Bosnia. It showcased the weak UN rules of engagement and demonstrated the need for more robust UN mandates for peacekeeping operations.

But the Danish action was not enough to change the UN's ways. The weakness of the UN led directly to the Srebrenica genocide, because the Bosniaks fled to the UN "safe haven" there, thinking that the UN troops would protect them. It was a fatal mistake. Speaking retrospectively, the later UN secretary-general Kofi Annan declared in 2005 that the UN had "made serious errors of judgment rooted in a philosophy of impartiality" in Bosnia, describing Srebrenica as a tragedy that would haunt the history of the UN forever.

The third lesson is that the United States is the only country capable of stirring the global community to decisive action. In that sense, the difference between Rwanda and Srebrenica is crucial. In Rwanda, as we have seen, the Clinton administration did everything it could to avoid taking action. By contrast, its reaction to the Srebrenica massacre was swift and decisive. Within days, Holbrooke was on the ground; within weeks, NATO planes were in the air; within months, a peace deal was on the table. None of that would have been possible without determined American leadership. The lessons of the genocide had been well learned.

Those lessons stayed with Clinton throughout his remaining time in office. The proof of that is in Kosovo, a province of Serbia with a majority Albanian population. In 1998–99, violence broke out between Albanians and local Serbs. President Milošević responded with great brutality and started a well-planned campaign of terror and expulsion of the Kosovar Albanians. This campaign could best be described as one of "ethnic cleansing" intended to drive the Kosovar Albanians out of Kosovo, destroy the foundations of their society, and prevent them from returning.

Once more, the United States shook NATO into action. In March 1999, American aircraft led a NATO bombing campaign against the Serbian forces threatening Kosovo. At the launch of the operation, President Clinton made very clear that he had learned the lesson of history: "In dealing with aggression in the Balkans, hesitation is a license to kill. But action and resolve can stop armies and save lives."

After seventy-seven days of air strikes, the Milošević regime was forced to accept a NATO-led international peacekeeping force in Kosovo (Kosovo Force, or KFOR) and to accept the province being placed under UN administrative mandate while a permanent solution could be found. The search for a solution lasted almost a decade; eventually, in February 2008, Kosovo declared independence and was recognized as an independent country by the great majority of Western states.

Today, there is relative peace and stability in the Balkans. The peacekeeping force in Bosnia is now managed by the European Union, and NATO's Kosovo peacekeeping force has been reduced from fifty thousand troops to less than five thousand troops, reflecting the significantly improved security situation in the region. In one of my meetings with the Serbian president, Tomislav Nikolić, he acknowledged that NATO today stands as a guarantor of peace and stability and the security of all people in the Balkans, a true success story.

At the end of the day, it was because of American engagement and leadership that the civil wars in the former Yugoslavia were brought to an end—even if that leadership came late. The Europeans had neither the ability nor the will to do what was necessary. The UN was hamstrung by indecision, and Milošević's forces were able to conduct a brutal campaign of ethnic cleansing until the United States finally and belatedly decided to act.

Had President Clinton not decided to act as a policeman

in the Balkans, Milošević and his brutal military commanders would have been able to continue their war crimes and violations of fundamental human rights, and, not for the first time in Europe's troubled history, the stability of the continent would have been threatened by the negative repercussions of the conflicts in the Balkans. The United States was the only power with the capacity, the decision-making power, and the political will to put a stop to the killings. It is fair to say that thousands of people across the former Yugoslavia owe their lives today to the actions of the American policeman in the 1990s.

The 2000s: Afghanistan and Iraq

It has become commonplace to lump the American campaigns in Afghanistan and Iraq together, and to present them as wars of aggression, reckless adventures that ended in unmitigated disaster. They are, in fact, widely viewed as proof that foreign intervention never works, and that America should give up trying to be the world's policeman and focus on problems at home.

But that interpretation is seriously flawed, especially in the case of Afghanistan. The US-led invasion of Afghanistan in 2001 was a question not of choice but of necessity. America had been attacked on 9/11; the man who planned the attacks, Osama bin Laden, had taken shelter in Afghanistan; the Taliban regime refused to hand him over. This was a hostile act, an act of war. The invasion was an act of self-defense, and fully justified.

The Iraq War, meanwhile, has become the symbol of interventionism devilry—almost the mother of all opposition to US military interventionism, with claims that the war was illegal, poorly prepared, and badly handled. Mistakes were, indeed, made in the conduct of the intervention—notably the failure to prepare a detailed and concrete plan for the reconstruction of the country and the reconciliation of its many ethnic and religious groups early enough. But I maintain that the Iraq War was legal and justified. Iraq's leader, Saddam Hussein, was a brutal dictator who would not abide by UN resolutions. His actions had to have a consequence, and for the people of Iraq, as well as the world community, it was a great relief to get rid of him.

Saddam Hussein rose to power in Iraq in 1979, a leading member of the revolutionary Arab socialist Baath Party. A Sunni Muslim himself, he became president and led a brutal dictatorship that suppressed all opposition, particularly Shia Muslim and Kurdish movements. His government was widely condemned for its systematic, widespread, and extremely grave violations of human rights and international humanitarian law; including summary and arbitrary executions; enforced and involuntary disappearances, indiscriminate jailing, torture, assassinations; and the use of terror against his own people.

In particular, Saddam had a proven track record of using weapons of mass destruction. In 1988, he ordered the use of chemical weapons against the Kurdish people in northern Iraq. The Iraqi army hit Kurdish areas with sarin and mustard gas. The attack killed between three thousand and five thousand people and injured seven thousand to ten thousand, most of them civilians. This incident has officially been defined as a genocidal massacre against the Kurdish people in Iraq. Saddam also ordered the use of chemical weapons against a popular uprising in southern Iraq in 1991, and during the war against Iran, the Iraqi military repeatedly used chemical bombs, artillery shells, and rockets.

When Saddam Hussein ordered the invasion of Kuwait, the UN Security Council responded by adopting Resolution 678, which authorized member states to use "all necessary means" to "restore international peace and security in the area." This provided the legal basis for the international military operation. After the Iraqis were driven out of Kuwait, and the Iraqi army was defeated, a cease-fire was signed. It was based on UN Resolution 687, which made the cease-fire conditional on Iraq meeting a number of requirements, including ceasing the use and development, and confirming the destruction, of chemical, biological, and nuclear weapons of mass destruction.

According to Resolution 687, Iraq was obliged to provide an "accurate, full, final and complete disclosure . . . of all aspects of its programs to develop weapons of mass destruction and ballistic missiles." To implement the resolution, Iraq was required to accept external scrutiny by international weapons inspectors. In the period from 1991 to 1998, the weapons inspectors destroyed large amounts of chemical and biological weapons. However, Iraq hampered the work of the UN inspectors, and in 1998 the UN had to pull the inspectors out of Iraq. As a result, a US- and British-led coalition initiated intensive missile strikes against Iraq in December 1998. This attack was legitimized by the still-existing UN Resolution 678, which authorized the use of all necessary means to ensure peace and stability in the region, as well as the violations of Resolution 687, which also was still in force.

In the subsequent three years, the Iraqi government denounced any kind of weapons inspection in the country.

Consequently, in November 2002, the UN Security Council adopted Resolution 1441, which stated that Iraq over the years had substantially infringed, and continued to substantially violate, its obligations under the agreed Security Council resolutions, including Resolution 687; it also stated that the violations constituted a threat to international peace and security. The resolution gave Iraq one last chance to fulfill its disarmament obligations, compelling Iraq within thirty days to present a full account of its weapons of mass destruction. However, Saddam Hussein did not live up to this resolution either, and on March 20, 2003, an American-led coalition launched an attack on Iraq.

As Danish prime minister, I supported the launch of a military operation against Saddam Hussein, and Denmark joined the international coalition, which numbered about thirty countries. It was a controversial decision that divided the European countries and domestically created strong opposition. Among other things, I was attacked with red paint by an outside activist inside the Danish parliament.

I supported the military action against Iraq because of Saddam Hussein's lack of cooperation with the UN. Saddam Hussein was given a last chance to cooperate, but he would not take advantage of the opportunity that a unanimous UN Security Council had given him to cooperate with the UN immediately, actively, and unconditionally. We knew that Iraq had previously produced and used chemical weapons. The Iraqi regime would not explain what had become of weapons that it had previously admitted being in possession of. This created considerable uncertainty in the region and internationally. Only through Saddam Hussein's active cooperation could the uncertainty about Iraq's weapons of mass destruction be removed. Therefore, cooperation was absolutely vital, and there was reason to be concerned about Iraq's refusal to cooperate. It was an aggressive regime that had invaded its neighbors and used chemical weapons against its own people.

The Danish military intelligence service did not have its own information about the possible existence of chemical weapons in Iraq. I noted that foreign services, including the American and British, seemed to believe that the Iraqi regime still had chemical weapons at its disposal, but as Danish prime minister I did not use the possible existence of weapons of mass destruction as an argument to join the international military coalition. For me, it was sufficient that Saddam Hussein had not adhered to and complied with UN resolutions. When a ruthless dictator so grossly violates UN rulings, it must have a consequence. Otherwise we are undermining the UN's authority.

In my view, there was a clear legal basis for a military operation in the already-adopted and applicable UN resolutions. Resolution 678 of 1990 authorized UN member states to use all necessary means, including military force, to enforce the Security Council's requirements and conditions. These requirements were further specified in Resolution 687 of 1991, which raised a number of conditions for the cease-fire with Iraq; and in Resolution 1441 of 2002, the Security Council had updated and confirmed the earlier decisions. The authorization to use force was therefore still valid.

My point was very clear: Whether or not Iraq possessed chemical weapons remained to be seen, but to avoid war it would be very easy for Saddam Hussein to eliminate any doubt by complying with the UN decisions and provide clear documentation as to whether Iraq had chemical weapons. In refusing to take that opportunity when it was offered, he had not only violated UN resolutions, but he had also created uncertainty about security in the region and internationally. For me, it was also important that the UN Security Council had repeatedly warned Iraq that "it will face serious consequences as a result of its continued violations of its obligations." If you are to ensure respect for UN resolutions, such warnings should also be followed up by actions; otherwise the UN will gradually evolve into a toothless forum that talks and talks, and does nothing.

Today we all know that chemical weapons were not found in Iraq in the wake of the occupation of the country. Obviously, that compromised the whole operation, because people had the impression that the main reason for the invasion was the existence of chemical weapons. The left-wing mantra became "Bush lied, people died." But as President Bush notes in his book, *Decision Points*, the charge was illogical: "If I wanted to mislead the country into war, why would I pick an allegation that was certain to be disproven publicly shortly after we invaded the country?" The fact is that intelligence agencies in the United States and around the world believed that Iraq possessed chemical weapons. As Bush notes, "Nobody was lying: We were all wrong." I know from numerous talks with George Bush that he was very angry about the misleading intelligence reports, and in *Decision Points* he is very clear about the political price: "While the world was undoubtedly safer with Saddam Hussein gone, the reality was that I had sent American troops into combat based in large part on intelligence that proved false. That was a massive blow to our credibility, my credibility, that would shake the confidence of the American people."

The fact that weapons of mass destruction were not found in Iraq does not mean that the basis for military action against Saddam Hussein was wrong. My decision was not based on secure evidence of Saddam Hussein's stocks of weapons of mass destruction; it was based on his lack of cooperation with the UN. Precisely because Saddam Hussein did not cooperate, there was a fundamental and unacceptable uncertainty about the illegal weapons he had. It was this unacceptable uncertainty that we had to deal with. The main questions were: Could we run the risk that a ruler like Saddam Hussein had these weapons and would use them? Should we give an unscrupulous and erratic dictator the benefit of the doubt? Could we accept that he, after twelve years of noncooperation, continued to express defiance to the UN Security Council? For me there was no doubt. Not only did we have the right to act, but it was our duty.

Hard Lessons in Afghanistan and Iraq

However, even though I believe to this day that we were justified in what we did in both Afghanistan and Iraq, the fact remains that serious errors were made in the follow-up to both campaigns. It is those errors, not the actual interventions, that led to the perception of failure.

In Afghanistan, there were three key errors that, while justified at the time, made things much harder. First, we put arbitrary deadlines for troop withdrawal, and that made it impossible for us to adjust to the situation on the ground. Second, we were too slow in building strong and credible indigenous security forces to gradually take over security. And third, we should have done more to help local authorities to build strong

THE WILL TO LEAD

institutions and develop good governance able to build trust between the people and the political leadership.

I have already discussed in chapter 1 the problem with our decision to set a calendar date for our withdrawal. That problem was compounded by the relative weakness of the Afghan forces when we withdrew, and that weakness was the result of our own late realization of the need to build them up. We did not start building up the Afghan security forces in earnest until 2009, the ninth year after the start of the military action. It was too late, and the hectic formation of the Afghan security forces that then ensued did not allow the depth and breadth necessary to construct a modern and strong security force fully capable of addressing a resurgence.

At the same time, our efforts for nation-building in Afghanistan were too weak and too reluctant. The truth is that the Western countries have been too reluctant to criticize the incredible inefficiency and the deep corruption of the Afghan government apparatus. It is probably a reflection of the usual Western self-criticism and self-doubt that led to the reluctance to do anything that could be construed as imposing our standards and requirements. But the result was that the poor governance itself led to distrust in the society at large, and to recruiting rebels to the Taliban and other terrorist organizations.

Therefore, the third lesson is that a military operation must be accompanied by a comprehensive political approach, a robust civilian effort to develop a modern and efficient local government administration. We should not refrain from setting reasonable conditions in return for our sacrifice in blood and treasure out of a misguided consideration for cultural differences.

This comprehensive approach should include a plan for economic reconstruction that advances economic growth after conflict by promoting free trade, entrepreneurship, and a market-driven economy. The problem is that the economy in war zones becomes tremendously dependent on the military forces and their centralized military planning: The army buys local food, employs local workers, and acts as a huge market for the local economy. When the military is withdrawn, the economic structures are either distorted or broken, the private enterprises have become very dependent on public contracts or subsidies, and the already poor communities have become even poorer as a result of war and conflict.

I believe that every major military operation should include an "Operation Wealth of Nation" with the aim to spur strong economic growth and job creation as quickly and efficiently as possible. A key ingredient in such a plan for economic reconstruction would be to promote the establishment of high-growth enterprises and to advance entrepreneurship, which is the engine of development. Security and economics are interlinked. It is a vital part of the reconciliation and post-conflict stabilization that people are able to experience economic progress and improved living conditions.

Our experience in Iraq, too, shows that the problem with interventions is not the military mission but the political follow-up. The problems began immediately after the fall of Baghdad and Saddam's flight. This created a political vacuum, and there were two decisions that in retrospect were probably not well considered. In order to ensure a clear break with Saddam, all officials belonging to the former Baath regime were removed, and the Iraqi army was dissolved. This meant that many Sunnis lost their jobs and took it as a signal that they had no place in the future of Iraq. Consequently, they joined the rebels who opposed the new Iraq.

However, it must be remembered that, after initial difficulties, we did manage to get Iraq back on track. The US troop "surge" in 2006–7 had a real effect on the ground. Following the surge, al-Qaeda–affiliated militias and death squads no longer swarmed the country, as they had just a couple of years before. US officials, state security services, tribal forces, and some armed groups had forged an agreement to work together against the most extreme groups terrorizing Iraq's population. The major roads in those areas were lined with the flags of the Awakening Councils—local fighters who had decided to protect ordinary Iraqis from al-Qaeda—and the Iraqi military was deployed in all major cities. Finally, Iraq had relatively good security, a generous state budget, and positive relations among the country's various ethnic and religious communities. The public had grown hostile toward al-Qaeda and other insurgent groups and were siding with the state and its army. It was a new atmosphere, and it was full of promise.

But the promise never materialized, and the sectarian violence increased after the withdrawal of US troops by the end of 2011. The withdrawal was envisaged by a security agreement reached between President Bush and Prime Minister Nouri al-Maliki in 2008. This so-called status of forces agreement (SOFA) was the legal basis for the presence of US troops in Iraq after the expiry of the UN mandate at the end of 2008. Thus, the continued US presence in the country after 2011 depended on its ability to negotiate an extension to the agreement with the Iraqi government.

The problem was that Prime Minister Maliki pursued an increasingly sectarian form of politics. He transformed Iraqi democracy into a Shiite majority domination that effectively marginalized Sunni communities in the country. This strained his relationship with the United States, which rightly criticized his actions, and despite the deteriorating security situation, Maliki refused to extend the security agreement. We all know that President Obama had campaigned on the promise to pull the United States out of Iraq, but even if he had wanted to, he could not have remained in Iraq because the Iraqi government refused to extend the security agreement. Despite initial plans to keep some forces in Iraq to assist the local army, no agreement could be reached between Washington and Baghdad, and the last troops pulled out in December 2011, leaving security in the hands of the often less than effective Iraqi military.

With US troops out of the country, Maliki reinforced his sectarian policies with a harsh crackdown against Sunnis in the country. Sunnis found themselves increasingly the victims of the Shia-dominated government security forces. In response, many Sunnis turned to the extremist Sunni insurgent groups, which eventually merged into the Islamic State. Indeed, the heavy-handedness of Iraq's army effectively acted as a "recruiting sergeant" for IS.

Again, the lesson of Iraq is that troop withdrawals should not be calendar-driven but conditions-driven, and that no military success will endure unless it is followed up by a successful and effective political reconciliation. Our mistake was not that we did too *much* militarily, it is that we did too *little* politically afterward.

The Reluctant Policeman: Libya

These lessons are clear with hindsight; the problem is that they were not clear at the time. By the time of the US presidential election in 2008, popular opinion in the United States had swung massively away from the whole concept of foreign intervention. President Bush's final approval ratings were among the lowest ever recorded, and while the Iraq and Afghanistan wars were not the only reason for that, they were certainly important factors.

That is the background to the decisive swing away from large-scale foreign intervention that marked the Obama presidency. Where Bush the younger was an enthusiastic advocate of America's role as the world's policeman, Obama was much more reluctant, only taking action where he saw he had significant foreign support. In fact, Bush believed in leadership, and was therefore able to act quickly; Obama believes in consensus, and therefore acted reluctantly.

Obama's role as the "reluctant policeman" was very clearly on show in his reaction to events in Libya in 2011. In February of that year, pro-democracy demonstrations against the dictator Mu'ammar Gadhafi began. The Libyan uprising quickly turned bloody as Gadhafi sought to suppress it with force. In March he massed troops around the rebel center, Benghazi, and having labeled his opponents "rats," he threatened the population, declaring, "We will show no mercy and no pity to them."

I was secretary-general of NATO at the time, and from the early stages of the crisis, I was in favor of international action to protect the Libyan people. However, when the UK and France offered a resolution in the UN Security Council calling for the establishment of a no-fly zone in Libya, they received little support for it, including from the United States.

The American position itself was unclear but seemed to show a reluctance to intervene. The then secretary of defense, Bob Gates, was the most outspoken against American involvement: "I believed that what was happening in Libya was not a vital national interest of the United States. I opposed the United States attacking a third Muslim country within a decade to bring about regime change, no matter how odious the regime."

At the same time as the French were lobbying actively for a military operation, they were equally active in opposing any NATO role. For instance, they told us that the Arabs were skeptical about NATO. This alleged Arab skepticism about the idea of NATO leading the operation was a false argument. In fact, the Arab countries were quite comfortable with contributing to the operation through NATO. They know NATO from our partnerships with countries in North Africa, the Middle East, and the Gulf; and throughout the process, I worked the phone to consult and to coordinate with countries in the region, and eventually to ensure their active contribution to a NATO operation.

The most remarkable telephone call took place on March 23. I had called the Turkish foreign minister, Ahmet Davutoğlu, to discuss the situation with him. I presented him with the French argument that the Arab countries were skeptical about a NATO operation in Libya. He rejected that, referring to his own talks with foreign ministers from the region, and added, "By the way, I'm just in a meeting with Sheikh Abdallah bin Zayed [the foreign minister of the United Arab Emirates] here in my office, and I'll hand over the telephone to him, so he can tell you himself." Sheikh Abdallah took the telephone and confirmed that the UAE would very much like to see NATO take the lead of the Libya operation, and he mentioned that other countries would have the same position. I got that confirmed in conversations with the Jordanian king, Abdullah, and the Qatari prime minister, Sheikh Hamad al-Thani; and while the secretary-general of the League of Arab States, Amr Moussa, couldn't commit on behalf of the member states of the League, he also confirmed in several conversations that he would be very comfortable with a NATO operation.

In fact, the contributing partners were all happy about the NATO lead. An interesting example was Sweden. It happened that I visited Sweden the day before a crucial vote in the Swedish parliament on Sweden's participation in the Libya operation. I met with the members of the Foreign Relations and Defense committees. The Social Democrats, who are known for their anti-NATO stance, told me, "Secretary-General, tomorrow we will vote in favor of Swedish participation in the Libya operation exactly because it is a NATO-led operation. NATO has the political and military structures that provide the political transparency and oversight that we demand."

So, one by one, the arguments against a NATO operation were removed.

Simultaneously, the US calculus changed. On March 13, 2011, the League of Arab States called for international intervention to halt the violence in Benghazi. The Arab League's unprecedented move was a game-changer because it meant that an international intervention would not be a Western-imposed solution but a locally backed one. This would not be a case of the West against an Arab state but of the world against a dictator.

In a decisive meeting with his security team on March 17, President Obama made the decision in principle that the United States should try to stop the killings. He set two important conditions: He wanted NATO to commit to leading the operation after a short initial phase, and he wanted UN Security Council backing for more robust military action if necessary—the authority to use all necessary measures to protect civilians.

All of a sudden, everything moved. The UN Security Council adopted the famous Resolution 1973, authorizing the use of "all necessary measures" to protect the civilian population in Libya. An international coalition was quickly established to enforce the resolution. The massive machinery of the US military and intelligence communities moved into top gear. France, the UK, and other allies began flying sorties over Libya, and the United States began a massive aerial and sea-based bombardment of Libya's air defenses and Gadhafi's forward forces in Benghazi. At the same time, the French objections to letting NATO take the lead melted away. Finally, after weeks of uncertainty in defining the role of NATO, the alliance was able to speed up preparations to take over the Libya operation.

On March 27, NATO launched Operation Unified Protector, taking command of air and sea operations around Libya. NATO provided the command-and-control backbone; allies provided the striking force. This was very much a multinational effort, built upon an absolutely essential American contribution. While Canada and the European allies conducted the majority of the strikes, the United States provided 75 percent of the intelligence, surveillance, and reconnaissance. It also contributed 75 percent of the refueling planes used throughout the mission and dispatched military personnel to reinforce the NATO commands with the necessary expertise. Seven months later, on October 31, the operation was completed.

The military operation was, by any measure, an indisputable success. But, as we have already seen (see chapter 1), and just as in Afghanistan and Iraq, the political follow-up was an abysmal failure. There was no leadership; there was no action. Libya was left to its own devices. We now know—thanks to the interview published in the *Atlantic*—that Obama expected French president Nicolas Sarkozy and British prime minister David Cameron to take the lead in the reconstruction, as they had in the buildup to the air campaign. Neither stepped up; nor did Obama.

As a result, our military success turned quickly into a political disaster. NATO faced accusations of destroying Libya, of removing Gadhafi and not having a plan to replace him—quite unjustly, because with no UN mandate NATO could not take action, and NATO is not a UN member. The NATO members who have permanent seats on the Security Council—Britain, France, and the United States—did nothing to push for international support for Libya until it was too late. America looked to Britain and France to lead; they looked to America; nobody moved. And while they hesitated, Libya fell into the abyss.

Fatal Hesitation: Syria and Islamic State

That perception of the Libyan operation as a failure is probably the main reason why it took so long for the United States to take action in Syria. In this terrible conflict, it is as if the horrors of Bosnia have repeated themselves on a much larger scale, with atrocities on the ground and hesitation on the part of the international community.

Syria's descent into self-destruction began at the same time as Libya's, in March 2011, and in the same way, with pro-democracy protests erupting against the regime of President Bashar al-Assad. His security services responded with a heavy-handed and self-defeating brutality that stood out even in that time of regional turmoil. Teenagers who painted revolutionary slogans on a school wall were arrested and tortured. When demonstrations broke out to protest against their treatment, the security forces opened fire, killing several demonstrators. The unrest triggered nationwide protests demanding Assad's resignation, and hundreds of thousands took to the streets across the country. The regime reacted by using ever more force in a bid to crush the dissent, but rather than breaking the protesters' resolve, it reinforced it—and radicalized it. Violence bred violence. Opposition supporters began to take up arms, first to defend themselves and later to expel the security forces from their local areas. The fighting escalated, and the country descended into civil war as the rebels formed armed brigades to battle government forces for control of cities, towns, and the countryside. According to the UN, 250,000 people had been killed by August 2015.

Atrocity piled on atrocity. The Assad regime used Scud missiles against civilian areas. His forces used barrel bombs and cluster weapons, which are illegal because they are indiscriminate. Extremists on all sides committed murders, mass killings, torture, and terrorism. In 2013, in the town of Ghouta, Assad's forces began using chemical weapons. Yet even though Obama had said that the use of chemical weapons would be a "red line" that would trigger an American response, he refused to order action. As we have seen in chapter 1, this refusal to act was disastrous. It gave the world the impression that the policeman had gone into retirement. Obama's hesitation, quite simply, was fatal.

And while Obama hesitated, the conflict deepened and broadened. The critical moment in this respect came in 2011–12, when an al-Qaeda leader in Iraq, Abu Bakr al-Baghdadi, decided to set up a branch of his terrorist group in Syria. Baghdadi's group, called the Islamic State in Iraq (ISI), had suffered a string of defeats at the hands of US and Iraqi tribal forces, and its expansion into Syria seems to have been as much a desperate gamble as a strategic plan, but it paid off. By 2013, Baghdadi's Syrian branch had built up a powerful battlefield presence, while ISI was once again carrying out dozens of attacks a month in Iraq; in April of that year, Baghdadi announced the merger of his forces in the two countries to create the Islamic State in Iraq and the Levant (ISIL).

By helping to destroy Syria, Baghdadi saved ISIL. The civil war allowed him to build up his forces, ready to take advantage of any opportunity for expansion, and that opportunity came in 2013, when a standoff between Iraq's Shia-led government and minority Sunni Arab community developed into a full-blown political and sectarian crisis. Baghdadi took full advantage of it: ISIL shifted its focus back to Iraq, exploiting widespread anger among Sunni Arabs against Maliki's sectarian policies. Backed by local tribesmen and former Saddam Hussein loyalists, the militants took control of the central city of Fallujah. Six months later, in June 2014, they launched an assault on Iraq's second-largest city, Mosul, to the north. Thirty thousand Iraqi soldiers dropped their weapons and fled when confronted by an estimated eight hundred gunmen. Emboldened, the militants advanced south toward Baghdad, massacring their adversaries and threatening to eradicate the country's many ethnic and religious minorities. At the end of the month, after consolidating its hold over dozens of cities and towns, ISIL declared the creation of a caliphate and changed its name to Islamic State (IS).

Yet still the international community hesitated, and without American leadership, nothing was done. There were many arguments in favor of inaction at that time: the lack of a UN Security Council mandate, the lack of support for military action from countries in the region, the sectarian complexities of the battle, the lack of a well-defined and coherent opposition that could have been the focus of support. Those reasons were, and are, all valid, but they were the sort of arguments that could have been overcome with patient diplomacy, energetic engagement, and determined American leadership. That leadership was simply not there, and no other country could provide it.

Only in August 2014, a full year after the Ghouta atrocity, did Obama finally authorize military action against IS. There is no doubt that this was the right decision: IS was on the verge of annihilating the Yazidi people, a distinct and independent religious community. IS had taken the city of Sinjar, massacred some five thousand Yazidi men, and sold a further five thousand to seven thousand women into servitude or handed them to jihadists as concubines. The terrorists were besieging an estimated fifty thousand more Yazidis on Mount Sinjar. The

United States asserted that IS's systematic destruction of the Yazidi people was genocide. The Arab League also accused IS of crimes against humanity.

At last, President Obama authorized targeted air strikes in Iraq against IS, along with air drops of aid. Eventually, US air strikes and Kurdish forces broke the siege. This was the beginning of an American-led international coalition carrying out operations against IS, which grew to include more than sixty countries. At the time of writing, the coalition has enabled Kurdish forces on the ground in Iraq and Syria to stem the relentless advance of IS and take back around 20 percent of the territory it had occupied. Without US leadership, the situation would have been much worse than it is. But if that leadership had been displayed two years earlier, it would have been much better.

The United States and Europe have paid an enormous price for this fatal hesitation. The war in Syria has turned into a strategic defeat for the United States, a strategic victory for Russia, and a threat to the cohesion of the European Union. While America and Europe talked, Putin acted recklessly to establish Russia as a power in the region and a player on the international scene, launching air strikes into Syria in September 2015. Those air strikes propped up the tyrannical Assad regime at the crucial moment and enabled its soldiers to retake lost ground at terrible human cost; they also weakened the most moderate, US-backed rebel groups, who then lost ground to both Assad and al-Qaeda.

Such decisive military action, with no attention paid to civilian casualties, allowed Russia and Iran to preserve and control the remaining puppet regime in Damascus. Russia's action pushed the surviving Sunni opposition forces closer to an alignment with Islamic State and other terrorist groups, and made it more certain than ever that this war will rage on and on. The regime's capture of Aleppo pushed tens of thousands more Syrian refugees toward a European Union already coming apart at the seams. For President Putin this is just another added bonus. He has hit two birds with one stone: enfeebled the United States and destabilized the European Union.

The Syrian disaster is an example of how conflicts can escalate out of control and develop into a broader threat when the United States hesitates. By any measure, Syria is a human tragedy and a great loss. Strategically, it is a calamity: an example that reckless autocrats and brutal terrorists will fill the vacuum when the United States and its allies retreat.

Yes, Only We Can

The record of history is clear: In Rwanda, Bosnia, and Syria before 2014, America hesitated, nothing was done, and the result was genocide. In Kosovo, Libya, and Syria after 2014, America acted, and genocide was prevented. Even Iraq and Afghanistan, so often cited as proof that intervention is not worth it, actually teach a different lesson: the danger of ending a mission before the job is done.

Taken together, I believe that this history of the past quarter century paints a clear lesson: Only the United States has the diplomatic, military, and economic power to provide decisive leadership and get things done internationally. Time and again over the past quarter of a century, we have seen that as long as the United States is in a state of doubt, holds back, and is undecided, there is no leadership, no direction, and no action. Once the United States gets its act together and provides leadership, things start to move and you can match words and action. To borrow from President Obama's own election slogan, it is not just "Yes we can" but "Yes, only we can."

Many Americans will argue, understandably, that this is not fair. After all, why would the Smith family in Peoria buy the argument that the United States should be the world's policeman? Wouldn't it serve US interests better to stay out of troublesome conflicts and leave it to the conflicting parties to resolve their own battles and entanglements? The brutal answer is that only superpowers have the necessary capabilities to get things done. The United States is the world's only superpower, and as Robert Kagan observed in the *New Republic* in May 2014, "Superpowers don't get to retire."

America's unique power takes many forms. The US military is unmatched in terms of economic resources, technological superiority, and capacity to deploy forces across the globe. The United States has an unparalleled ability to build alliances, underpinned by a strong worldwide corps of skilled diplomats. No other country in the world has the strength to complete the task as a global policeman, and the UN, which would be the natural alternative, is too weak. It is rare that the United Nations decides to take military action, and when that happens, member states often refuse to make the necessary military equipment and personnel available, and limit the use of the assets to a point that makes the UN impotent. Now that Russia—a UN veto-holder—has apparently decided to base its foreign policy on opposing the United States at every turn, the prospects for an active and engaged UN are worse than ever.

On top of this, I am convinced that the majority of people in the world have more confidence in the United States than in other potential candidates for the role of global policeman. China is a rising power, but without economic and military strength to pursue a global role as policeman. What is more, China is a Communist dictatorship that would be met with skepticism in many countries. Russia would like to challenge the US leadership, but Russia is a nation in decline, and the country's assertive attitude toward her neighbors has developed a global distrust in Russia's intentions.

By comparison, the United States is a benign democracy pursing democratic ideals of freedom rather than territorial interests. Therefore, America is also an appealing community that has attracted talented people from across the world. They are enticed by her wealth, respect for universal values, and open-minded approach to the world. The American melting pot has infused into the United States a diversity that has established networks all over the world and generated an interethnic confidence in the United States. So the world needs a policeman, and there is no one other than the United States to do the job. To be the policeman of the world is an awful, thankless job, but someone has to do it, and the United States is the only nation that can.

In fact, the argument that America should retreat, retrench, and pull up the drawbridge has two fundamental flaws. For one thing, it is morally repugnant. This is not a policy of handing the solution of problems to somebody else: It is a problem of handing them on to nobody, of letting bad things happen, and standing idly by. As we have seen, Bill Clinton did that in Rwanda in 1994. He still bears the moral scars.

The second reason is that those who want America to stop being the world's policeman and start being their own gatekeeper seem to believe that if America stays away from the troubles of the world, the troubles of the world will stay away from America.

That creed seems to forget the horror and shock of 9/11. The harsh reality is that America, by virtue of its physical size and strength and its ideological attractiveness, will always be the subject of resistance, or even hostility and hatred, from the forces in the world that will challenge America's undeniable and exceptional supremacy, or simply hate the principles of freedom and the way of life that are the foundation of the United States and its allies of liberal democracies. There is no reason to believe that terrorist organizations like Islamic State or al-Qaeda, for instance, would refrain from trying to strike American citizens or interests in the United States or overseas, even if the United States were to retreat and only mind her own business. America is the world's top power, and in many parts of the world it is also the top regional power. That means that any country that wants to take the top spot for itself will feel that it has to knock America down, regardless of the way the United States behaves.

So whether the United States withdraws from world affairs or not, the United States—and American hegemony—will be the target of terrorists, rogue states, and resurgent states, either through direct attacks on the United States and American interests or through attempts to undermine the US-led world order. Adversaries will attempt to damage and weaken the United States. In the extreme case, they will threaten the safety and security of individual American citizens, as we saw on 9/11.

That's the destiny of being a superpower. And the new technology, a globalized world, and new ways of travel and communication mean that America is no longer protected by two great oceans. The bad guys can strike anywhere at any time, even in the American homeland. So if the United States does not go out into the world to nip the evil at the root, the evil may strike in the United States. So it is indeed in America's own interest to take leadership and act as policeman.

It is clearly the most effective and least expensive approach to knock down conflicts and threats while they are still small. If the United States is reluctant to be proactive in due time, there is a risk that the skirmishes and menaces will grow too large and require disproportionate resources to fight. If you stand idly by and let conflicts, menaces, and atrocities run out of control, it may require the deployment of large troop forces for a long time to handle the situation. But if you nip it in the bud, before troublemakers grow too strong, threats can be tackled by targeted precision operations that are limited in time, scope, and resources. And you can further reduce the American costs by building alliances and partnerships and carrying out the job in collaboration with like-minded nations.

In many ways, the theory and practice of "the broken window" also applies to world affairs. The theory of "the broken window" is well known: If a broken window is left unfixed, it sends a signal of disorder and can lead to more serious problems. A broken window tells criminals that the local community doesn't have the will to defend against criminal invasion. Conversely, if broken windows are fixed, and if there is zero tolerance for disorder, this approach sends a signal that criminal behavior is not tolerated. This in itself may prevent major crime. This strategy was implemented with great success to clean up New York City in the nineties. The same applies to the international community. If a breach of the international order remains unpunished and unfixed, it sends a signal of a lack of will and ability to defend against violations of international law. This can lead to even more and greater international disorder as terrorists and aggressors decide that there is little risk of retribution. In that sense, too, there is a need for a policeman to monitor the international security situation and send the signal that violations of international law will not be tolerated.

It is a vital US interest to protect the rules-based international order against erosion. That order—built, as we have seen, under Truman's visionary leadership after World War II—has served the world well, but it has also facilitated American interests in a world dominated by free trade and peaceful coexistence within a rules-based institutional framework. When resurgent states, rising states, or terrorist organizations challenge this world order, they are also challenging the rules and principles that allow American business and the American people to prosper. American ships sail the world's seas, American tourists travel the world's countries, American companies invest in the world's industries, American consumers buy the world's goods, and the "Made in the USA" label is in high demand across the globe. All of that has been made possible by the rule of international law.

We must remember that this liberal and rules-based world order is not a divine, God-given phenomenon but a system of freedoms that was imposed on the world by the United States after World War II, thanks to the overwhelming US strength and foresight, and which can only survive if an invincible strength is maintained to defend it. America made it; America benefits from it. America stands to lose the most if it is overthrown.

And there are those in the world who do seek to overthrow it. Putin and others want to replace the liberal and rules-based order with their own vision: a world in which the strong and violent give the orders, and the small, weak, and peaceful obey them. The United States stands to lose many times over if that is allowed to happen—lose in security, in alliances, in market access, in its diplomatic power. In other words, the vital interests of the United States go far beyond narrow self-defense.

This was the message of President Roosevelt when he asked the American people to defend "not their homes alone, but the tenets of faith and humanity on which their churches, their governments and their very civilization are founded." It was the message of President George H. W. Bush when he spoke in defense of "a world where the rule of law, not the law of the jungle, governs the conduct of nations." It was the message of Secretary of State John Kerry when he said, "You just don't, in the twenty-first century, behave in nineteenth-century fashion." All of these statesmen knew that there are people and powers in the world who would love to behave in exactly that way, and it is only the fear of US power that stops them from doing it.

This is why the American people have a vested interest in taking on global leadership and doing the job as the world's policeman, despite the hardship: America prospers when the world is at peace and the rules are respected. But since there will always be malignant actors who want to break the rules and breach the peace, and since one successful example of rule-breaking will inevitably encourage a dozen others, America has to be able to demonstrate the strength and willpower to deter aggressors, prevent conflict, and keep together the international order.

In retrospect, perhaps the greatest value of the past seventy years of US hegemony is what did not happen: the wars that never broke out, or were not allowed to spread, because there was a policeman to put them down in time. It may be hard to calculate the value of these wars that never happened, but the value is there in every moment of peace and prosperity the American people have enjoyed. The cost of action is more visible than the benefits of deterrence, but as we all know, prevention is better and cheaper than treatment.

CHAPTER 6

AMERICA AND EUROPE
A Necessary Partnership

Those who cannot remember the past are condemned to repeat it.
—GEORGE SANTAYANA

I n July 1994, my wife and I took our children on an "educational journey" to Normandy, France. That year we commemorated the fiftieth anniversary of Operation Overlord, the Allied invasion of Nazi-occupied France. D-Day launched the armies of the United States, Britain, and Canada, together with forces in exile from France, Poland, and many other European nations, in the decisive battle against the Nazis in Europe. It was a brilliant and daring operation that, at the cost of thousands of lives, sounded the death knell for the Nazi empire in the West.

On this July day in 1994, the invasion beaches were an image of peace and tranquillity. There were even holiday-makers and swimmers enjoying the sun, sand, and sea on Omaha Beach, the deadliest of the landing zones, where the sand was ripped up by bombs and bullets and colored red by blood on June 6, 1944. However, we were not there for leisure, but to remember the brave soldiers who, fifty years earlier, had sacrificed so much for our freedom. We drove from beach to beach, remembering the famous names: Sword, Juno, Gold, Omaha, Utah. At the descent to every beach there is a monument to the brave men who paid the ultimate price in the landings.

As a Dane, I was proud to find a Danish monument located a few hundred yards from Utah Beach. It pays homage to the eight hundred Danish sailors who, although they did not land on the beaches, contributed greatly to the success of the D-Day landings. On June 6, 1944, thirty-one Danish ships, twenty-four of them flying the Danish flag, took part in the landings under British command. But the many war cemeteries made the strongest impression, one that we will never forget: the thousands of white crosses in straight rows, a testimony to the huge losses that the struggle for freedom cost.

Seventeen years later, I had the great honor to meet some of the veterans of World War II. As secretary-general of NATO, I attended the commemoration of Victory in Europe day on May 8, 2011, at the national World War II memorial in Washington, DC. Few of those veterans are still with us, and they are getting on in years, but if they can, they still show up to commemorate the end of the most brutal and devastating war the world has ever seen. In my remarks I paid tribute to the veterans: "You defended the freedom of Europe. You made it possible for future generations to enjoy peace and democracy. We thank you." I cannot but deeply respect and honor the burdens and sacrifices carried by the United States and its people to promote freedom, preserve peace, and create better opportunities for mankind at this, the most pivotal and dangerous moment in human history.

But in my speech, I not only paid tribute to the brave servicemen and women who fought their way across Europe not to subjugate it, but to give it back to the forces of democracy and freedom: I drew the lesson of the conflict, because it seemed to me that to forget that lesson is to risk throwing away the very gains they fought and died for. A saying attributed to Spanish American philosopher George Santayana runs, "Those who do not learn from history are doomed to repeat it," and for me, the lesson we have to learn from our history is clear. As I said in my memorial speech: "The Second World War brought home what we should have already known: that the security of America and Europe is indivisible."

It would be tempting to view the two great oceans that flank the United States as a defense against any adversary, but it would simply be wrong. Two generations ago, the Japanese attack on Pearl Harbor, the subsequent German declaration of war on the United States, and the bellicose German maritime operations in the Atlantic made it crystal clear to the Americans that the two oceans were no protection at all. And the Nazi blitzkrieg and rapid occupation of most of Europe made clear to the American people that the rise of an authoritarian hegemon on the European continent could threaten core US security interests as well as vital US economic interests. If Hitler had been allowed to consolidate his hold on Europe, the United States would have been confronted with a formidable enemy on the other side of the Atlantic—challenging America's control of the Atlantic sea-lanes themselves.

The same insight guided the American efforts to protect Europe from the Soviet Union during the Cold War. Had the United States not provided security and economic assistance to the ruined Europe in the wake of World War II, Europe could have easily fallen to the Communists, and America would have been confronted with another authoritarian and threatening hegemon on the other side of the Atlantic.

This stark lesson of history has guided decades of US foreign policy: The best way to keep the Atlantic and North America safe is to keep Europe strong, stable, and friendly. The countries of Europe are America's strategic neighbors, and no matter how frustrated Americans may grow with their behavior at times, it is better to invest in keeping the neighbors strong and stable than to risk instability or the advent of a hostile power.

Instability or the rise of a hostile power may seem far-fetched, but it is not unthinkable. The great difference between the United States and Europe is that the states of the United States are united; the states of Europe are not. Europe is a collection of small and middle-sized countries that have spent centuries fighting one another. They only learned to cooperate over the past seventy years, and they were largely able to do so because of the strong US commitment to their security. It was US-led initiatives such as NATO and the Marshall Plan that allowed the countries of Europe to break the murderous habit of conflict and work toward stability, freedom, peace, and democracy. Europe is peaceful and prosperous today because America helped it become so. But America cannot afford to take its hand off the wheel. Europe is not yet a stable structure: It is a club of diverse states that are being shaken by diverse forces, from racism and anti-Semitism to far-left and far-right extremism. And many of those forces would love to dissolve the club altogether.

If the United States were to disengage, there is a significant risk that the European Union would disintegrate, and disintegration would breed disaster. At the very least, Europe would lose all semblance of unity. It would once more be a collection of small and medium-sized states arguing over internal issues and incapable of acting together on the world stage; and the power vacuum left by the retreat of America and the rejection of Brussels would be filled by a resurgent Russia, whose aggression has already been felt in Georgia and Ukraine.

I am not suggesting that Russia would physically occupy Europe, but it would find it easier to influence the policies and economies of individual European countries, even the largest. By leveraging its control of key countries and, in particular, the extreme European dependency on imported Russian gas, Russia could effectively turn Europe into an expanded Russian sphere of influence. In this situation, the partnership between the United States and Europe would be history. Politically, the United States would lose a valuable European partner, and in terms of security, the United States would be faced with a strengthened, assertive Russia that has already made anti-Americanism the central plank of its foreign policy and is seeking out anti-American forces across Europe with which to build an alliance.

———

THE AMERICAN PEOPLE should not forget that Europe is still divided between those forces who favor an alliance with America and those who want to create a geopolitical alternative to the United States. Any signal of American disengagement, not to speak of a pivot away from Europe, strengthens America's enemies and weakens its friends.

Ever since the end of the Second World War and the creation of the great international institutions under the leadership of the United States, powerful elements in European political and intellectual elites have dreamed that the European nations could form a more cohesive whole to counterbalance the United States. When President Dwight D. Eisenhower undercut Great Britain and France during the Suez Crisis in 1956, German chancellor Konrad Adenauer famously told French prime minister Guy Mollet, "France and England will never be powers comparable to the United States; not Germany, either. There remains to them only one way of playing a decisive role in the world: That is, to unite Europe. We have no time to waste. Europe will be your revenge."

Chancellor Adenauer was a pro-Atlanticist; he just described a reality. But the idea of creating a European alternative to America, rather than an alliance with America, has persisted into our own times, and at times it has provoked serious rifts within the European family of nations.

The most striking recent example came in the buildup to the Iraq War in 2003. Opinions in Europe were bitterly divided, and French president Jacques Chirac and German chancellor Gerhard Schröder not only regularly criticized the US approach in outspoken terms, but also claimed to be speaking on behalf of Europe as they did so. Chirac, in particular, made his opposition to the United States a central plank of his worldview.

Jacques Chirac is a fascinating personality. He is well versed in French history and culture and a strong defender of the French language. Once he left a European meeting when one of his compatriots, a businessman, spoke English, claiming,

"This is the language of business." Having spent some time in the United States, Chirac speaks excellent English himself, but it is a matter of principle with him to defend the French language against what he sees as Anglo-Saxon linguistic imperialism. Being former French minister of agriculture, he not only is an expert in every nook and corner of EU agriculture policy, but also has a veneration for agriculture, farmers, and rural life, and was often seen campaigning in the countryside. In the French village where my family and I have a vacation home, there is a saying that Jacques Chirac has patted every cow in France. A typical French *élégantier*, he also understands courting the women. I think my wife has a hidden admiration for the former French president since he, in the typical French way, courteously kissed her hand.

I always enjoyed talking with President Chirac, but his worldview differed profoundly from mine. During a working lunch, he once told me, "The American approach is simplistic and influenced by the fact that the United States is a young civilization." That statement reflects an American-skeptic sentiment frequently met within the political, intellectual, and media establishment in Europe, sometimes even a kind of anti-Americanism. Chirac also showed little regard for the smaller countries of Europe. He once attacked Eastern European countries, saying they "missed a good opportunity to be quiet" when they signed letters backing the US position on Iraq.

On several occasions, Chirac repeated his vision of a multipolar world, in which there would be an American pole, a European pole, a Chinese one, an Indian one, and eventually a South American pole. He once told me, "It is dangerous when the United States tries to impose her thinking on others. France has, together with Germany, Russia, and China, another, but common vision, and the four countries are speaking with each other." He and Chancellor Schröder met frequently with Russian president Putin, and both before and after the Iraq War they forged a kind of alliance against the United States. When Schröder was voted out of office, he even went to work as a lobbyist for the controversial Nord Stream gas pipeline from Russia to Germany that he had approved as chancellor.

I saw this vision of a French-German-Russian alliance as a dangerous geopolitical fantasy that would weaken not only the transatlantic bond between Europe and the United States but also the solidarity and cohesion of the European Union. I also strongly opposed what I considered President Chirac's attempts to undermine and weaken the prime minister of Great Britain, Tony Blair, who certainly did not share Chirac's vision of a multipolar world with Europe setting itself up in opposition to America. On the contrary, he was in favor of a very strong bond between Europe and America to tackle problems together.

To understand the role America can and must play in Europe for its own good, it is worth considering Chirac and Blair as the two poles of geopolitical thinking in Europe. If Jacques Chirac exemplified the dream of a European alternative to the United States, Tony Blair exemplified the realism of an alliance.

I cannot remember a single case when I disagreed with Tony Blair. He was the first to call and congratulate me when I was elected prime minister in 2001. Soon after, he hosted a meeting in Downing Street, London, where, over breakfast, we laid the foundation for several years of close cooperation. We had very close and frequent contacts. Once, in the preparation for a press conference in Copenhagen, I told Tony Blair that some media in Denmark insist that I'm in his pocket. "Yes, and they claim I'm in George Bush's pocket; and he is in the pocket of the Almighty," Tony said as he completed my sentence. At another time, I communicated with Tony while canoeing down the St. Croix River on the border between Minnesota and Wisconsin. Having celebrated our son's marriage to Kristina Smith from Minnesota, we were preparing a canoeing trip when Downing Street called with a request for a phone conversation. We equipped one of the canoes with communication tools, including a satellite phone, started paddling down the river, and just before the agreed time for the telephone call, we found a quiet sandbank in the middle of the river. We got ready for the telephone call. I got Tony on the line, and we started our discussion. Suddenly he stopped and asked me, "Anders, I hear the singing of birds and the purl of water. Where are you?" I told him where and why, and, laughing, he said, "I envy you. I wish we could transform such personal transatlantic bonds into strong political ties between Europe and the United States."

Coming from two different political parties, we nonetheless shared common positions on international politics, European politics, and even domestic politics. In 1999, Blair gave a great foreign-policy speech in Chicago in which he made the case that humanitarian military intervention can sometimes be necessary to save lives and protect human rights against assaults by ruthless dictators. He was a pronounced exponent of an ethical foreign policy. He pushed strongly to intervene militarily in Kosovo in 1999 to prevent a looming genocide, and he engaged Britain in a military operation to save lives in the African state of Sierra Leone, for which he won genuine applause. But he was heavily criticized for his support of the Iraq invasion in 2003.

I have no doubt that he thought from the first that military intervention was the morally correct course to follow, and he firmly believed that a special relationship between Great Britain and the United States, and indeed between Europe and the United States, was essential for the protection and promotion of the values of freedom and democracy. Even in the face of negative public opinion he stood firm and steady, and you could always count on him. He was a strong leader, but eventually he was forced to step down. It is a rich British Labour Party and a rich British nation that can afford to throw away such a stout and gifted leader. And Europe needs political leaders who are devoted both to European integration and to the alliance with the United States. That's exactly why President Chirac saw Tony Blair as a major obstacle to his vision of Europe as a contrast to America.

Indeed, at a crucial moment in the Iraq debate, Tony Blair was one of the leading spirits behind an op-ed article that eight of us European leaders—Blair; Prime Ministers José Maria Aznar of Spain, Silvio Berlusconi of Italy, José Manuel Barroso of Portugal, Péter Medgyessy of Hungary, and Leszek Miller of Poland; the president of the Czech Republic, Václav Havel; and I—signed, to refute the claim by Chirac and Schröder that they were speaking on behalf of Europe. Under the headline "United We Stand," the article appeared on January 30, 2003, in the *Wall Street Journal* and a number of European newspapers. It was a broad statement of support for the United States in its efforts to put the maximum pressure on Saddam Hussein to comply with the UN Security Council resolutions. "The solidarity, cohesion and determination of the international community are our best hope of achieving this peacefully. Our strength lies in unity. . . . The transatlantic relationship must not become a casualty of the current Iraqi regime's persistent attempts to threaten world security," we wrote.

It is a rare event for so many national leaders to take our peers to task in public, but the situation was extremely grave. Chirac and Schröder were not only putting themselves on a collision course with the United States, they were trying to drag us along with them. We wanted to emphasize that there was no European consensus on the Franco-German criticism of the United States. It was my clear view that a rift between Europe and America would be a weakening of the international community that would reduce pressure on Iraq and play into the hands of Saddam Hussein. For me it was also a question of the fundamental solidarity within our transatlantic alliance: Allies help each other when needed. Europe owes its freedom to the United States, which has helped the Europeans both in older and more recent history; then Europe should also help the United States when called. "Thanks in large part to American bravery, generosity and far-sightedness, Europe was set free from the two forms of tyranny that devastated our continent in the twentieth century: Nazism and Communism," we wrote.

In the end, Europe remained divided. Many of us joined the US-led campaign in Iraq; France, Germany, and a few other countries did not. But at least we avoided an open rift between Europe and the United States, which could have had serious geopolitical consequences.

The lesson of this painful episode is that America has both friends and would-be rivals in Europe. There are still politicians on the Old Continent who would prefer to see Europe as a competitor to the United States rather than a partner, and no matter how illusory that dream is, they will seek to make it reality. Europe still has its Blairs and its Chiracs, and if America does not stay engaged and show its support for the Blairs, it will run the risk of seeing the Chiracs steer Europe away.

When European integration bolsters Europe as a strong partner of the United States, it is good for freedom, peace, and prosperity. But if Europe sets itself up as a counter pole to the United States, it will only weaken the forces of freedom and strengthen the autocrats, including Russia. Hence, from a geopolitical and security point of view, the United States has a core interest in staying strongly engaged and cultivating its allies and partners in Europe. We cannot afford to lose our alliance to the forces of continental drift.

———

GIVEN THAT EUROPE is a collection of small and medium-sized states in a dangerous neighborhood, whereas the United States is a superpower with secure borders all around, it is always more likely that America will have to help Europe than the other way around. Many Americans therefore ask why they should keep on investing American lives and American wealth in Europe's security.

The first point is that the United States has a vital economic interest in strong ties with Europe. Actually, these ties are mutual, as Europe and the United States are each other's biggest trade and investment partners. The economy of the European Union is as large as that of the United States, and its population of 510 million is considerably larger than America's 320 million. The EU is the world's largest trading bloc, and it ranks first in both inbound and outbound international investment. The EU is also the top trading partner of eighty countries.

The formation of an economically unified Europe has accelerated European economic growth and development, and this has opened trade and investment opportunities for the United States. Combined, the EU and the United States generate about 40 percent of world gross domestic product, and their mutual trade accounts for about half of all world trade. Mutual investments are huge: US investment accounts for about half of the total foreign investments in the European Union, while investment from EU countries accounts for over 60 percent of the total foreign investment in the United States.

So, from an economic point of view, Europe is an indispensable partner of the United States. Notwithstanding current challenges stemming from the refugee crisis, the debt burden, negative demographics, and rigid societal structures, the countries of Europe hold a lot of potential that could be further advanced through strengthened transatlantic cooperation.

Germany is an economic powerhouse with a strong manufacturing industry and strong competitiveness. France has a number of large international corporations that are world leaders in their field, and France pursues a global approach to defense and security. The UK is a global financial center and has a global perspective through the Commonwealth. Italy is rich in culture, fashion, and links to strategically important North Africa. Eastern Europe is reform oriented, with enormous growth potential. The transformation of the former Communist states into modern democracies and vibrant economies has generated impressive growth rates, jobs, and prosperity and created a region with huge future opportunities. Despite exorbitant tax rates, the Nordic countries have combined a social welfare system with efficient market economies. Stout free traders, they rank high in international evaluations of competitiveness, doing business, protection of property rights, and lack of corruption.

The same is true in terms of security. While no other country on Earth can boast the military power of the United States, countries like Britain and France still punch above their weight in terms of hard power. Even smaller countries, such as my own Denmark, can make a big contribution to multinational military operations.

Above all, Europe and North America bring their security concerns together in NATO. For almost seven decades, NATO has ensured the security and stability that have allowed all of our nations to flourish. With its unique integrated command structure, unrivaled military capabilities, tried and tested forces and procedures, and extensive network of partnerships, NATO is the most successful alliance in history. America has alliances with other countries in other parts of the world, but only in Europe does it have the standing capability that NATO can provide. That is something that is worth preserving.

———

HOWEVER, WHILE GIFTED with a lot of opportunities, the European Union is teetering on the brink of disintegration, not only because of the current refugee crisis but, more fundamentally, because of endemic weaknesses, such as negative demographics, rigid labor markets, inadequate welfare systems, and the debt burden. Whereas an appropriate response to most of these challenges would be profound reforms of

European societies and a more outward-looking Europe, there is a clear risk that nationalistic, inward-looking forces will gain ground and push Europe in the direction of more closed societies and less engagement with the world beyond the continent.

Such developments would run contrary to fundamental American interests. The United States has an essential interest in keeping Europe as a vital, vigorous, and vivid partner and ally; an ally that is capable and willing to help America protect and promote the principles of freedom and democracy. And Europe has a core interest in maintaining an American commitment to transatlantic economic and security cooperation. But Europe needs a shot in the arm to remain the strong, preferred partner that the United States needs to carry out the task of being the world's policeman. To that end, Europe must reform itself, and on both sides of the Atlantic, political leaders and civil society must engage in preparing a wide-ranging plan for creating a strong and integrated transatlantic community. That will require strong and sustained efforts to deal with the migrant and refugee crisis, stimulate economic growth, liberalize markets, and encourage trade.

The greatest threat to European unity is the current refugee and migrant crisis. Indeed, the massive influx of people fleeing war, oppression, and poverty threatens to shatter Europe, breaking up the European Union and the unity that was the core of the new regional order that visionary European politicians, supported by the United States, created after World War II. The recent vote in the United Kingdom to leave the European Union is an expressive demonstration of the centrifugal forces that are now threatening to fragment Europe.

More than one million migrants and refugees crossed into Europe in 2015, the result of the worst migration and refugee crisis since World War II, as people fled conflict and poverty, primarily in the Middle East, Africa, and Afghanistan. Forging common EU measures has proved difficult because of national sovereignty concerns and the asymmetrical impact of each migrant crisis. The states of first arrival are keen not to end up bearing the burden alone. The transit countries are tempted to divert the flow of migrants to other nations by selectively closing their borders and, if that is not possible, to pass the refugees along to the next country as rapidly as possible. The countries where most refugees ended up wish to slow down the inflow and call for EU-wide burden sharing.

The inflow of refugees and migrants is likely to continue for years, and probably decades. Not only Syria but also a number of other Middle Eastern countries are facing security challenges that could give rise to new refugee flows. More and more Afghans are aiming to leave their increasingly unstable country. Growing migration pressure can also be expected from Africa, due to poverty and a steadily increasing population.

The likely high levels of immigration into the EU in the coming years could bring both benefits and challenges. On the one hand, an aging Europe will need qualified immigrants to ensure future economic growth and financing of the European welfare systems. On the other hand, overly rapid and uncontrolled inflows could exceed the capacity of the host countries to integrate the new arrivals and finance education and social services. If the European Union cannot deliver on securing its external borders and ensuring fairer burden sharing among member states, a progressive renationalization of not only migration policies but also other policies will be unavoidable. The likely outcome will be not only stagnation but fragmentation.

Such a development would be a deadly blow to decades of efforts to create a new Europe, whole, free, and at peace. It is absolutely essential to counter this destructive development and to bring Europe back on track. The problem is overwhelming. To fix it, there is a need for groundbreaking reforms, nationally as well as at the European level, that will challenge much European conventional thinking. However, this is such a daunting task that the United States and Europe should address it in a joint effort. While the societal structures of America and Europe are different, we are facing the same challenges, and those challenges could have a considerable impact on the future of our liberal democratic societies and the transatlantic relationship. That is why we need a transatlantic refugee and immigration policy.

Such a policy should have as its foundation the firm belief that people who uprooted themselves, fled their country of birth, and made the risky and dangerous journey to America or Europe possess a lot of initiative, drive, and courage. These are people who feel compelled to succeed in their new country because they left so much behind in their old country. Many of them have an entrepreneurial spirit. It is no coincidence that 40 percent of today's Standard and Poor's companies in the United States were founded by immigrants or their children. These immigrants want the chance to live, to work, and to prosper. The challenge in both the United States and in Europe is to give them that chance.

Doing so would benefit the whole of society, through the energy and entrepreneurship the new arrivals bring, but it would demand a united effort by all the host countries. To make sure that our countries stay true to the principles of the open society and do not fall prey to xenophobic populists, I would suggest a five-point plan in a joint American-European effort to address the refugee and immigrant challenges:

First, we should make the newcomers to America and Europe an asset and not a liability for our societies. Essentially, we should liberalize access to work and restrict access to social benefits. An open society is open to workers, not to welfare abusers. Too often, refugees and immigrants have difficulties getting a foothold in society because it is too difficult to get access to work and too easy to get handouts from the government. It would be fair to say that people who come to a new country cannot be eligible for social assistance until they have stayed, worked, and contributed to the community for at least a number of years. Such a system would also make it easier for people to accept the free movement of labor across borders.

Second, it is indispensable to establish a tight, impenetrable external border control, including effective vetting rules and procedures to prevent potential terrorists from entering our countries. This is the first prerequisite to better manage the influx, and a better controlled inflow is necessary to ensure an adequate integration of the newcomers, both in America and in Europe.

Furthermore, effective external border controls are an absolute prerequisite for maintaining freedom of movement across internal EU borders. If there is no confidence in the external border, country by country will introduce national border controls. That would be a huge economic setback for Europe. The way forward is a common, EU-controlled external border control. While the EU is a relatively loose union of sovereign nation-states, the United States is a relatively strong federal state. Perhaps the EU could draw inspiration from the United States on how federal border controls are operated. This would initially encounter opposition from individual European nations, but it is essential; otherwise, the EU will disintegrate, possibly with a small, hard core of countries that will bind each other closely, with the rest of the EU in a looser community.

Third, there is a need for fair burden-sharing, both within Europe and between Europe and the United States. So far, the United States has only accepted a tiny proportion of the refugees, and it should accept a much higher number. The treatment and handling of refugees is a joint responsibility. We can't just turn our backs on people who are fleeing from President Assad's chemical attacks, Russia's random bombing of civilians, and IS's beheadings and crucifixions. Basic human decency requires us to find solutions to the fate of these unfortunate people.

However, we also have to be realistic. Neither America nor Europe will be able to accommodate all the wretched of this world who seek refuge and a better life. After having agreed on an allocation between the United States and the EU, we should help the conflict zones' neighboring countries to receive and accommodate refugees and finance the burden. We should put maximum pressure on the wealthy nations in the region to accept more refugees and help finance the task. And overall, Europe and America should do more to help fragile states in the near neighborhood, creating a positive economic and social development, so that their citizens seek better opportunities in life at home rather than desperately embarking on the hazardous journey to Europe and America.

Fourth, Europe and America will need robust policies for returning illegal immigrants to their countries of origin. This should be complemented by well-run and well-regulated channels for legal migration. In order to counter the people-smuggling industry, applications for asylum or work permits could be processed in third countries, and accepted asylum-seekers or migrants could be brought directly to America and Europe, undercutting the illegal and repulsive business of human trafficking.

Fifth, it is essential to do away with the naïveté of integration policies. We must realize that successful integration is much more than providing jobs and training for newcomers. There is also a need for values-based education to promote values-based integration. For a successful integration, it's crucial that new arrivals with a sometimes radically different cultural and religious background understand and respect the historical, cultural, and religious roots of our societies and the values upon which our civilization is built. For example, immigrants should make the effort to learn the language of their host country—a basic principle, but one that is not always observed and causes great resentment when it is ignored.

More important still, immigrants must understand and accept our attitude to religion, and the way in which religion and the state interact. This is particularly important for the hundreds of thousands of Muslims fleeing to Europe, who come from a different tradition in which the roles of religion and state are blended very differently, and who have a strong cultural identity in which their religion often plays a central role. While Americans, generally speaking, are more religious than Europeans, there is in America a very clear separation of church and state. Religion is a private matter, and you have a strong, religious civil society. In some European countries, such as France, there is a strict separation between church and state, *la laïcité*. In other countries, the separation is not quite as sharp, but all over Europe, it is a clear foundation for democracy that legislation is decided by the elected parliament and not determined by holy scriptures.

While of course there are differences from country to country, America and Europe are basically influenced by the Enlightenment ideas of individual human rights, which gradually evolved into demands for equal rights for women and men, equal protection for all religious beliefs and sexual orientations, and the subordination of church and religion to the state authorities.

Freedom of religion, as well as freedom of expression, are integral principles of our liberal democracies. Each individual has the right to practice his or her religion freely, and freedom cuts two ways. The right to practice your religion freely is complemented by the right to have a free and critical religious debate. Freedom of expression cannot be abolished or limited by claiming that something is holy, and therefore exempt from discussion.

In essence, newcomers to Europe and America might not like the fact that European citizens and the media can criticize figures whom they view as holy, but they have to accept it, because the law that protects such critics is the same law that protects the migrants themselves. Opponents of this approach will claim that it is a form of cultural imperialism aimed at imposing our values when, in fact, it is about preserving and enforcing our laws. The law applies to all citizens equally. The law that protects freedom of expression is the also the law that protects you against discrimination on any grounds, such as sex, race, color, language, religion, political or other opinion, and national or social origin. For successful integration, it is essential that new citizens understand and respect these fundamental rules.

How we handle the refugee crisis will be crucial for the future of Europe, America, and, indeed, our liberal democratic values. Europe is under siege. The arrival of hundreds of thousands of immigrants and refugees is already testing the cohesion of the European Union and, indeed, Europe at large. It is leading more and more Europeans to question what the benefits of European integration actually are. For America, an unraveling of the European Union would be a major blow to decades of efforts to build a Europe whole, free, and at peace. If the tide is to turn, Europe has to act. In order to regain trust and optimism, Europe needs to be revitalized. It needs a shot in the arm.

———

THE GOOD NEWS is that Europe has a strong potential to once again become the continent of optimism and growth, and remain a solid partner of choice for the United States. And the United States can help that European renaissance by working to reinforce security cooperation within NATO and to boost economic cooperation with new agreements.

Security and economic growth are inextricably linked. Since 1949, NATO has been the framework for security cooperation between North America and Europe. The most famous clause of the North Atlantic Treaty is Article 5, which states that an attack on one ally is an attack on all, but it is worth remembering that before that comes Article 2, which states that the allies will seek "to eliminate conflict in their economic policies and will encourage economic collaboration between any or all of them."

Few people are aware of the existence of Article 2. When the treaty is mentioned at all, it is most often in the context of Article 5. That needs to change. We need a new transatlantic relationship in which our economic cooperation is as close and consistent as our security cooperation; what could be called a relationship of "Article 2 plus 5." Confronted with the new geopolitical challenges, the assertiveness of resurgent states, and attempts to undermine the rules-based international order, North America and Europe should enhance and expand the transatlantic relationship into a truly "integrated transatlantic community."

An integrated transatlantic community would help us to strengthen the different strands of our relationship: our security cooperation, our economic links, and our personal ties. It would help us to protect our common values, our populations, and our societies; to promote the rules-based international order and norms and practices; to preserve our peace and our prosperity; and to assist other nations' progress toward peace and prosperity, too.

As a top priority, we must continue to strengthen the security strand, because security is the foundation for everything that we have and everything that we hope to achieve. After decades of détente in Europe, a resurgent and aggressive Russia has created a fundamentally new security environment on the European continent. This will require a new NATO security posture.

This work has already begun. NATO is establishing a persistent presence in the Eastern European countries most exposed to Russia, in the form of a continuous rotation of troops. In addition, and based upon a proposal I made after Russia's annexation of Crimea, NATO countries have set up a spearhead force at constant high readiness, to be deployed within a few hours. But more must be done. If Europe wants to be a useful and preferred partner for the United States, European allies must also make their military forces more deployable, and acquire military assets that make them able to assist in international operations beyond Europe.

But as we all know, nothing comes for free, and security certainly doesn't. That's why it is vital that NATO remains fit for that purpose—not for the sake of war, but for the sake of peace. All allies must continue to invest in NATO, politically, militarily, and financially, and all must shoulder a fair share of the burden, just as all share in the benefits, including living up to the NATO benchmark of defense investments equivalent to at least 2 percent of GDP. That commitment is a key part of a truly integrated transatlantic community.

However, credible deterrence is not only a question of the size of investments and the amount and quality of military capabilities. It is as much a question of the willingness to actually use these capabilities if needed. In 2015, the Pew Research Center published a survey that revealed a highly disturbing lack of will to defend friends and allies with armed force. The Pew Center asked the following question: "If Russia got into a serious military conflict with one of its neighboring countries that is our NATO ally, do you think our country should or should not use military force to defend that country?" In Germany, 68 percent responded no to this question; in France and Italy, 53 percent and 51 percent, respectively, answered no.

The fact that a majority are against the use of military force to defend an ally is in direct contradiction to the very foundation of NATO. Article 5 builds on the oath of the Three Musketeers: One for all, all for one. If this solidarity is questioned, it is the very raison d'être of NATO that fades away. Fortunately, the answers in the survey are not reflected in the stances of political leaders. While, for instance, 68 percent of the Germans seem to be against the use of military force to defend an ally, I feel sure that German chancellor Angela Merkel, who, due to her upbringing under Eastern German Communism, is firmly committed to the defense of freedom, would never hesitate to help allies, even with the use of military force. But the depressing result of the Pew survey is the need for determined political leadership to cultivate and maintain the sense of solidarity and the commitment to a robust defense of our values. Security is precious, and freedom is priceless, but neither comes for free: We have to be able and willing to defend both.

Like NATO for security, we also need an "economic NATO." The ultimate goal should be to create a transatlantic free trade area (TAFTA). A transatlantic free-trade zone would bring enormous benefits to all of our nations and all of our people for generations to come. It could set a new gold standard in economic cooperation, just as NATO has long been the gold standard in security cooperation. And just like NATO, it could be a strong pillar for a truly integrated transatlantic community.

The first step could be a rapid conclusion of the negotiations between the United States and the European Union on the Transatlantic Trade and Investment Partnership (TTIP). The long-term benefits of a successful TTIP would be enormous. It would boost trade and investment; it would stimulate jobs, innovation, and growth; and it would promote the principles of a rules-based trading system.

Of course, we are all aware that there are vested interests and sensitivities over a wide range of issues such as agricultural subsidies, genetically modified organisms, chlorinated chicken, public health, and sanitary regulations. But while we should respect legitimate concerns, we should not let particular interests and sensitivities undermine the much greater good that we can achieve for all of our nations and for the rest of the world. The greater strategic good should not be bogged down with technical details.

———

STRENGTHENING TRADE AND economic activity across the Atlantic is an important priority, but my vision for an integrated transatlantic community is much broader. It's also about strengthening people-to-people relations, and promoting the values and ideals that we all share. I believe that students, academics, and artists should all have greater opportunities to cross the Atlantic in both directions. Comprehensive exchange programs of greater cultural, educational, and scientific cooperation will help to strengthen our community of values, and it will also underpin TTIP.

But there is more to this than just traditional exchange programs. The regular interaction between businesspeople and other professionals across the Atlantic is of invaluable importance to continuously nurturing the economic, political, cultural, and personal bonds as well as strengthening shared values. In Europe, we know how much it impacts on common European policies that leaders from all walks of life from all over Europe meet frequently in Brussels. The same positive effect across the Atlantic is essential if we are not only to uphold but also to reinforce the transatlantic relationship.

I know how much I benefited from traveling to the United States as a young politician some thirty years ago. It gave me a profound understanding of the country and its people, and it created bonds with families, colleagues, and institutions that I still cherish today and that continue to help me in my work.

In 1982, I traveled to the United States as a guest of the International Visitor Leadership Program. The IVLP is the US Department of State's premier professional exchange program. Through short-term visits to the United States, current and emerging foreign leaders in a variety of fields experience the United States firsthand and cultivate lasting relationships with their American counterparts. Visitors from all over the world have come to the United States, they have learned about American society, they have met Americans from all walks of life, and they have established warm friendships with families across the country. Many visitors have later become leaders in their own countries, leaders in politics, business, or in other fields. They carry with them a deep knowledge of American history, culture, and way of life, and some wonderful memories from their visit to the United States. You can't overestimate the importance of that investment in a deeper cultural understanding.

My trip to the United States in 1982 was the first time that I had ever visited the country. The travel program was an exploration of American geography, culture, and political ideas. I spent a bit more than a month in the States, during the second half of the stay accompanied by my wife. I traveled from Washington, DC, to Syracuse in upstate New York, to Chicago, Dallas, Minneapolis, Phoenix, San Francisco, and New York City before going back to Europe. We established personal bonds with families who accommodated us in their private homes, we helped a farmer in Minnesota bale straw, visited Danish American communities in Wisconsin, drove through the impressive Nevada desert, and looked out over the staggering Grand Canyon. I participated in political meetings; I spoke with citizens, politicians, academics, and businesspeople; I attended a rodeo; I shook so many hands that I almost believed that I was running for office myself; and I found Americans to be very much like the people in my native Jutland: kind, hospitable, and often skeptical of government. I learned a great deal, and I ended the trip more convinced than ever that the United States and Europe share a unique bond that must be preserved and strengthened.

———

THERE IS ONE AREA where, in particular, Europe can and should work more closely with the United States to solve one of the world's most dangerous problems: the Israeli-Palestinian conflict. But to play a useful role, Europe will have to come to terms with the darkest part of its history and culture: anti-Semitism.

In April 2004, I visited Houston, Texas, and brought with

me a special gift to the local Holocaust museum: a model of the Danish cutter *Elisabeth K571*. It was carved from timber from the actual cutter, which was used to rescue Danish Jews from Nazi persecution during World War II. Thanks to the courage of my compatriots at the time, most Danish Jews were smuggled across the strait between occupied Denmark and neighboring neutral Sweden, where they found refuge. It is estimated that some 95 percent of Denmark's Jewish population survived the war. For that deed, the Houston Holocaust Museum wanted to reward the Danish people, and as prime minister I went to Houston to accept the Lyndon B. Johnson Moral Courage Award on behalf of Denmark.

In my acceptance speech, I stated: "The organized persecution and unprecedented systematic attempt to exterminate the Jewish people, its culture and traditions, is a shameful and indelible stain on European history." That is as true today as it was then, and the more I consider that history, the more I am ashamed to see how anti-Semitism, often disguised as criticism of Israel, has again started to be expressed in Europe.

Since the founding of Israel in 1948, Israel and the West have enjoyed a unique and strong relationship. The history of the Holocaust and common perceptions of shared democratic values have contributed to strong bilateral ties. Today, Israel is a vibrant economy and well-functioning democracy, one of relatively few countries in the world deemed "free" by the independent monitoring organization Freedom House. That is all the more remarkable when you consider that Israel lies in a region plagued by turmoil.

But in spite of this positive track record, Israel is increasingly the object of European criticism and loathing. In 2013, a BBC

World Service global survey found that Israel was the fourth most "negatively viewed" nation in the world, after Iran, Pakistan, and North Korea. In only one Western country—the United States—did a majority express favorable views of Israel. Out of EU nations, the UK was found to have the most unfavorable view: 72 percent of the Brits surveyed felt negatively about Israel, and in France the number was 63 percent.

Anti-Semitism and resentment toward the State of Israel have inflamed hatred and violent acts against Jews across Europe. The US State Department declared in 2014 that Europe was witnessing a wave of anti-Israel sentiments that crossed the line into anti-Semitism. Attacks on synagogues and raids on Jewish shops have become a part of everyday life for many European Jews. The dividing line between anti-Israel and anti-Semitic sentiments is, at times, diffuse. Deep-seated anti-Semitism in Europe can have the effect that many leaders are quick to condemn Israel, yet take their time to utter a word of condemnation of terrorist attacks conducted by Palestinians. One example is the European silence when the Palestinian Authority president, Mahmoud Abbas, in a television speech on November 16, 2015, stated, "We bless every drop of blood spilt for Jerusalem. With the help of Allah, every martyr will be in Heaven." He added, "Al-Aqsa is ours, and so is the Church of the Holy Sepulchre. They have no right to desecrate them with their filthy feet." The European Union didn't hold Mahmoud Abbas to account over his incitement to violence and his unwillingness to condemn the ongoing stabbing attacks.

Today, many people have forgotten why Israel was established in the first place. Often we hear the question, "Why could Jews just come and occupy Palestinian land and drive out the Palestinians already living there?" Apart from all the religious connotations, some historical facts are crucial to understand this complicated situation. The State of Israel was founded with support from the international community in the wake of World War II. There was widespread recognition that the Jewish people needed a homeland after centuries of exile and persecution culminating in the Holocaust. On November 29, 1947, the United Nations recommended the partition of Palestine into two states, one Jewish, one Arab. The UN resolution followed a 1922 decision by the League of Nations to grant Britain a mandate over Palestine, which included, among other things, provisions calling for the establishment of a Jewish homeland facilitating Jewish immigration and encouraging Jewish settlement on the land. The Jews accepted the United Nations resolution while the Arabs rejected it. When the British mandate over Palestine expired, on May 14, 1948, the Jews proclaimed the creation of the State of Israel. The United States recognized the new nation on the same day, and the Soviet Union soon followed suit.

This is obviously a case with many dilemmas. Evidently it's not without problems to establish a new Israeli state on a territory hitherto occupied by Palestinians. On the other hand, it was crystal clear after the atrocities against the Jewish people during World War II that Jews must have their own land where they could build a new future, and where would such a nation otherwise be located? We must remember that there were already hundreds of thousands of Jews living in Palestine, and the fact is that Israelis and Palestinians could have lived peacefully together if the Arab countries had initially accepted the UN resolution on the partition of Palestine.

Anyway, Europe has a strong case—I would say an obligation—to support Israel. First, there is the historical legacy. The Nazi crimes against the Jews created a special debt to the Jewish people that should be redeemed through an unequivocal European support for the idea of an Israeli state that could defend itself against attack. History taken into account, it is commendable that German political leaders are very aware of Germany's special ties with Israel. But it would be a mistake to believe that this is solely a German obligation. The fact is that the Nazis had helpers in many European countries in their attempt to exterminate the Jews. I hate to say it, but the fact is that anti-Semitism has always lurked under the surface of European culture. Given Europe's troubled history at this point, it has a special obligation to support Israel.

Second, Israel is a free society living up to the high standards of a true democracy. Despite being attacked by their neighbors several times since the establishment of the State of Israel, and despite living in constant fear of terrorist attacks, the Israeli people have managed to build and maintain a stable democracy with a lively political debate, a vibrant media environment, and protection of civil rights, notwithstanding indispensable security measures. I would guess that more Palestinians enjoy democratic rights inside the State of Israel than in any other place in the region.

Democracies should unite and support each other to protect and promote the principles of freedom and democracy. In the choice between autocracy and democracy, you can't stay neutral. In a sea of civil wars, terrorism, and political oppression, Israel stands as an island of stability, freedom, and democracy.

European countries should support Israel to demonstrate to countries in the region that freedom and democracy pay.

Third, Europe should pursue a more balanced approach to maximize its influence over all parties in the Israeli-Palestinian conflict. Europe has lost much credibility among Israelis because of its bias against Israel, and has not won credibility among the Palestinians in return. The only viable solution to the conflict is to establish a two-state model, as envisaged by the UN in 1947 and advanced on several later occasions, most recently by President George W. Bush in 2002. It is a precondition for a viable two-state solution that a Palestinian state is economically viable and sustainable, and that the State of Israel is guaranteed security. The vision is of two states, Israel and Palestine, living side by side in peace, harmony, and security. Europe's best chance to promote this vision would be to support Israel, be friends with Israel, and, against that backdrop, request that Israel ensure the sustainability of an independent Palestinian state by stopping the illegal settlements that undermine the viability of a Palestinian state. At the same time, the European Union should tell the Palestinian people that Europe will always support freedom and democracy, peace and security, and that the Palestinians can count on European support provided they guarantee Israel's security, stop terrorism, and establish a true democracy in Palestine.

The Israeli-Palestinian conflict is a tragedy for Israelis and Palestinians, for the Middle East at large, and also for Europe, which is suffering from the wars, conflicts, and instability in the immediate neighborhood. Israel is a democratic beacon, a stable society, and a vibrant economy in a region that desperately needs freedom, democracy, stability, and economic prosperity. If Israel and its neighbors could come together in peace and harmony and establish friendly contacts and fruitful trade relations, the region could release its untapped potential, create wealth, jobs, and prosperity, and form a virtuous circle in which economic progress could generate more stability, less conflict, more collaboration, and even more progress. The Mediterranean could again become a sea of peace, where the refugee flows could be replaced by the flows of merchant ships, creating strong and positive economic relations and people-to-people relations between Europe and the Middle East and North Africa.

———

EUROPEANS, IN GENERAL, feel a strong bond with America. The broad European popular admiration of, trust in, and support for the United States provide a very solid foundation for building an integrated transatlantic community. While some elitist groups within the political, academic, and cultural establishment occasionally express anti-American sentiments, that's not reflected in the attitude of the man in the European street. It is striking that there is a considerable distance between the anti-Americanism that can be encountered in some parts of the political and intellectual elite, and how the general public admires and feels attracted to America.

On a regular basis, the Pew Research Center publishes surveys on America's global image, and according to the latest survey, from 2015, America's image in European populations was largely positive, with around two in three having a favorable opinion in Italy, Poland, France, the UK, and Spain. The outlier is Germany, where only 50 percent gave the United

States a positive rating, while 45 percent expressed a negative one. America's image in Germany has grown more negative in recent years, no doubt mainly because of the National Security Agency spying scandal, which was seen in Germany as a gross violation of German laws and a pattern of behavior more suited to the Communist-era secret police. In France, there is a stark contrast between the political elite and the average citizen: Three in four of the respondents expressed a favorable attitude to the United States, while you often meet anti-Americanism or at least a strong America-skepticism within the political, cultural, and intellectual elite.

In order for Europe to reach its full potential, Europeans should get rid of the last remnants of anti-Americanism, and America should help by promoting further military cooperation, further economic integration, and further people-to-people contacts. For Europe, there is no future in a multipolar world in which Europe acts as an alternative to the United States, simply because Europe would be squeezed between global centers of power that have both greater strength and greater geopolitical will to pursue their strategic goals. Different centers of power will inevitably become rival centers of power, which would be dangerous and destabilizing. Europe's best chance is to act in a strong and equal partnership with the United States, help build an invincible global liberal democratic hegemony, and support the United States in exercising determined global leadership of a unipolar world that favors freedom. And America's best chance of keeping the eastern shore of the Atlantic stable, safe, and friendly is to keep on working with the countries of Europe.

CHAPTER 7

RUSSIA AND CHINA
The Spoilers

The demise of the Soviet Union was the greatest
geopolitical catastrophe of the century.
—PRESIDENT VLADIMIR PUTIN

Barely had I been seated before Vladimir Putin told me
that NATO no longer had any purpose and should be
dissolved. "After the end of the Cold War, we dissolved
the Warsaw Pact. Similarly, you should dissolve NATO. That
is a relic from the Cold War," he said.

While he was speaking, I observed his contentious body
language. He likes to be seen as a strong man, and at that
moment, he seemed to be looking for a fight. We all recall the
macho posturing of Mr. Putin with a judo black belt, Putin
riding horses and fishing in wild rivers, often shirtless, or Putin
in helicopter rides with camera crews over the wide gray tundra,
looking for tigers and bears. He claims to have an ascetic and
modest mode of life, with just a spartan apartment and a couple
of cheap cars declared as his official fortune. Characteristically,
he—in contrast to the Soviet-era leaders—has had neither
statues erected nor ships or streets named after him. In a way,

I think he feels a bit bored in the grandiose and ornate halls of the Kremlin, but on the other hand, they are also a potent symbol of power and a strong, powerful man. This is how he would like to be seen.

I knew Putin from many previous meetings, so I was prepared for a very direct conversation. I told him that my ambition was the exact opposite of his: namely, to strengthen NATO as the bedrock of Euro-Atlantic security. Then we embarked on a quite rigorous and detailed discussion about missile defense and arms control in Europe. The date was December 2009; it was my first visit to Moscow as NATO secretary-general and chairman of the NATO-Russia Council, a cooperative body the NATO members and Russia had founded in 2002. Putin was prime minister at the time, and I also had the opportunity to meet President Dmitry Medvedev and Foreign Minister Sergey Lavrov. Upon taking office as secretary-general in August 2009, I made it one of my priorities to strengthen cooperation between NATO and Russia, and that included visiting Moscow just a few months into the job. I hoped that Medvedev, the newly elected president—a younger, more liberal, and more Western-oriented politician—would infuse more positivism and dynamism into the NATO-Russia relationship. But while Medvedev was polite, Putin was brusque and dismissive. I realized it would be uphill work to make any progress.

Since then, things have gone downhill. Russia, which began the millennium with such great promise as a partner and colleague of the Western democracies, has turned aside from that path. Instead, it has taken the path of autocracy at home and aggression abroad, trampling on the Russian people's rights to democracy and the rule of law, and bullying the international community with threats, blackmail, and outright violence. Russia is not the greatest power in the world—it is not even a superpower—but its actions make it the greatest threat to the proper working of the international order. China is the superpower of the future; Europe is America's indispensable partner of the future; but Russia is the future's problem child, and the next US president will have to find a way of dealing with it.

It did not have to be this way. Indeed, I regard it as one of the great tragedies of the post–Cold War period that Putin evolved from a pro-Western democratic reformer to an anti-Western autocrat. The first time I met him was on May 28, 2002, in Rome, on the occasion of the NATO-Russia summit, which took place at the Pratica di Mare Air Base, in an impressive setup prepared by Prime Minister Silvio Berlusconi. In Rome, we met a very pro-Western Putin. I still remember his speech during our working lunch, where he made the case in strong terms that Russia and the West should strengthen cooperation, and he looked forward to working closely with NATO on an equal footing. I left Rome very optimistic, and convinced that we were now entering a new era of cooperation between Russia and our Western organizations, NATO and the European Union.

But six years later, in stark contrast to the spirit of Rome, I met a very angry, hostile Putin in April 2008 at the NATO-Russia summit in Bucharest. He almost lost his temper, accusing NATO of encircling Russia, warning Ukraine and Georgia against joining NATO, and declaring that if Ukraine were to join NATO, it could bring the state to the brink of dissolution. In the animated exchange that followed, he also claimed, "Kiev remains the mother of Russian cities." He left Bucharest in a fury, and a few months later, in August, he sent an unmistakably clear signal to the West by invading Georgia and occupying the two breakaway regions of Abkhazia and South Ossetia.

What happened between 2002 and 2008 to make such a difference? First, what made Putin so Western-oriented in 2002? At the summit in Rome, we made the ground-breaking decision to found something very special—the NATO-Russia Council—as a mechanism for consultation, consensus-building, cooperation, joint decision, and joint action. NATO's member states and Russia would work as equal partners on a wide spectrum of Euro-Atlantic security issues of common interest. This was a remarkable step in the relationship between Russia and the transatlantic alliance, and it made the NATO-Russia relationship truly unique, because Russia is the only country outside NATO with which we have such a council. After the end of the Cold War, the collapse of the Soviet Union, and a decade of searching for a new Euro-Atlantic security architecture, we took a visionary step forward, inviting Russia to join us in a close partnership.

Leading up to the Rome summit, the relationship between the United States and Russia had seen huge progress, not least in the wake of the 9/11 terrorist attack on the United States. President Putin was one of the first foreign leaders to call President Bush, express sympathy and solidarity, and declare strong determination to cooperate in the fight against terrorism. President Bush pursued an engaged personal diplomacy with Putin, culminating in a joint declaration in May 2002 on a "new strategic relationship between the United States and the Russian Federation." I still remember my first meeting with President Bush in March 2002. Bush said to me, "I know that some of our folks in the Pentagon still consider Russia an enemy, but I have looked into the eyes of Putin, and I saw a friend." Even in retrospect, I think that was an accurate picture. At the time, President Putin pursued pro-Western policies. He even hinted at a possible future Russian membership of NATO, when asked by the BBC if it would be possible for Russia ever to join NATO, saying, "Why not? I do not rule out such a possibility—I repeat, on condition that Russia's interests are going to be taken into account if Russia becomes a full-fledged partner." On October 4, 2001, he elaborated further in the *Moscow Times* under the headline, "Putin Softens Stance on NATO."

The tragic events of 9/11 were a stark reminder of the need for comprehensive and coordinated action to respond to common threats. In a joint statement on September 12, 2001, NATO and Russia expressed their shared anger and indignation at the barbaric attacks on the United States and called on "the entire international community to unite in the struggle against terrorism." The allies and Russia were quick to recognize and seize the opportunity to boost NATO-Russia cooperation. Two meetings between President Putin and NATO secretary-general George Robertson, and meetings of NATO and Russia foreign ministers, paved the way for the important decisions at the summit in Rome.

So, in 2002 it seemed that Russia and the West were on the path to engage in close and positive cooperation. However, events in Georgia and Ukraine in 2003–4 dramatically changed the cooperative environment. So-called color revolutions in the two countries brought new, democratic, and pro-Western leaders to power in Tbilisi and Kiev. In Georgia, the Rose

Revolution led to the election of the young, energetic Mikheil Saakashvili as president, and in Ukraine, the pro-Western Viktor Yushchenko became president after the Orange Revolution. In Moscow, President Putin followed these events with great anxiety. He was convinced that the West in general, and the United States and the CIA in particular, had instigated and orchestrated these revolutions, and that the ultimate goal was to pave the way for similar regime change in Moscow. He saw conspiracy everywhere, and from that moment he changed his strategic calculations and turned increasingly anti-Western.

The upheavals in Georgia and Ukraine were truly revolutionary—modern revolutions based on hope and optimism, not blood and torment. On November 23, 2003, the president of Georgia, Eduard Shevardnadze, was forced to resign. After disputed parliamentary elections, he had attempted to open the new parliament. Two of the main opposition parties considered the session illegitimate. Led by Mikheil Saakashvili, supporters of those two parties burst into the session with roses in their hands (hence the name "Rose Revolution"), interrupting a speech by President Shevardnadze and forcing him to escape. The next day, the president announced his resignation, new elections were held, and Saakashvili became the new president of Georgia.

The Orange Revolution was a series of protests and political events that took place in Ukraine from late November 2004 to January 2005, in the immediate aftermath of a presidential election that was alleged to have been marred by massive corruption, voter intimidation, and direct electoral fraud, and in which Putin had campaigned personally on behalf of one of the candidates, Viktor Yanukovych. Nationwide protests succeeded when the results of the original elections were annulled and a revote ordered by Ukraine's Supreme Court. Viktor Yushchenko was declared the official winner of the new elections, and with his inauguration in January 2005 in Kiev, the Orange Revolution ended.

The pro-Western governments of Georgia and Ukraine aspired to become members of NATO. As a first step, they applied for a Membership Action Plan (MAP) and pushed for it to be granted at the NATO summit in Bucharest on April 2, 2008. Their pro-Western governments saw the MAP as a counterweight to the pressure from Moscow. After some deliberations in the Washington interagency process, President Bush decided to support their applications for the MAP: "If these two democratic states want MAP, I can't say no" was his principled stand. As prime minister of Denmark at the time, I supported that position, and so did the United Kingdom and the eastern members of our alliance. The Central and Eastern European states felt strongly about this issue and saw the NATO response as a litmus test of the West's will to defend the interests of the former Soviet territories.

But approval required unanimity, and both Chancellor Angela Merkel of Germany and President Nicolas Sarkozy of France were skeptical, in particular because they were worried that NATO could be drawn into a conflict with Russia due to the tensions between Moscow and the two countries. They were also concerned about corruption and the lack of political stability in Georgia and Ukraine. Both concerns were relevant. However, I still think Russia would have been less likely to engage in aggression if these countries had been on the path into NATO. As for the governance issues, a step toward membership would have encouraged Georgia and Ukraine to clean up corruption and improve governance. My experience of several rounds of NATO and EU enlargement has shown that the possibility of membership acts as a powerful incentive for reform.

When the summit started, this crucial issue had not been resolved. It is rare that such important matters are not worked out beforehand, and it made the summit charged from the beginning. It ended up as one of the most intense and engaging summits I have ever attended. Usually, our officials have precooked the items on the agenda, and as political leaders we can focus on the overall strategic perspectives and finally nail down the agreements. But this meeting was different. I will never forget the interactive negotiations in the meeting room, when we suspended the formal meeting and Chancellor Merkel called the Central and Eastern European leaders over to a corner of the room. Raised in East Germany, she knew well the sentiments of the former Communist states. She was sensitive to the legacy of Germany and felt a special responsibility to facilitate the process toward a Europe united, free, and at peace. She did something quite remarkable and savvy: She sat down in the middle of the group of leaders and did concrete drafting of a possible summit agreement, word by word. Finally, we agreed on a compromise. We would not grant Georgia and Ukraine MAPs in Bucharest, but we would issue a statement announcing that they were destined for future membership in NATO: "Ukraine and Georgia will become members of NATO," it said. In a way, it was a paradox: A MAP is no guarantee of future membership of NATO, but having denied them a MAP, we nevertheless stated that they will become members of NATO in the future.

This statement added to President Putin's anger. In the NATO-Russia meeting, he made statements that, seen in hindsight, were a forewarning of the later Russian aggression against Georgia in August 2008 and against Ukraine in 2014. He started out by expressing concerns about the NATO enlargement policy in general, and then addressed Georgia and Ukraine in particular. He emphasized that Georgia was involved in a centuries-long ethnic conflict with the Abkhazians and South Ossetians, and that these ethnic conflicts would not be solved if Georgia were to enter NATO, and he more than hinted that Russia would approach these ethnic conflicts the same way that the West had handled Kosovo—that is, it would eventually recognize their independence. On Ukraine, he was even more aggressive. He declared that Ukraine is a complicated state due to the fact that one-third of the population is ethnic Russian. Ukraine was created by receiving huge territories from Russia in the East and from Poland and Romania in the West. He indicated that Ukrainian membership in NATO might lead to the dissolution of the Ukrainian state. He also made some comments on Crimea that we did not take sufficient notice of at the time. In Crimea, he said, 90 percent are Russians, and he suggested that the 1954 decision to transfer Crimea from Russia to Ukraine was illegal because that decision was merely made by the Communist Party Politburo without following formal state procedures.

———

BUT PUTIN'S EVENTUAL drive to autocracy and aggression was not caused solely by the revolutions next door. In his annual State of the Union address in 2005, he declared, "First and foremost, it is worth acknowledging that the demise of the Soviet Union was the greatest geopolitical catastrophe of the century." This statement reflected what gradually evolved to become Putin's ultimate goal: to restore Russian greatness. A key element is to establish a zone of Russian influence in the "near-abroad," which is more or less equal to the former Soviet Union.

There are three myths that, in a decisive way, affect the thinking of Putin, as well as those in the Kremlin and Russians in general: the humiliation, the betrayal, and the conspiracy.

First, many Russians felt humiliated by developments in the 1990s—the loss of land in the Baltics, Central Asia, the Caucasus, but especially Ukraine, and the economic chaos and political turmoil during the Yeltsin years. While most Russians did not miss Soviet Communism, the events of the 1990s are not remembered for a positive opening of society after decades of dictatorship. Instead, they are remembered with shame as a period when Russia allowed herself to be humiliated.

Second, there is the feeling of betrayal. It is a widespread myth in Russia that the West made a pledge in 1990 during negotiations on the reunification of Germany. According to the Russians, Western negotiators promised that NATO would not expand eastward. The truth is that such a promise was never delivered. The documents from these negotiations have been declassified recently, so we can see clearly what was said, and what was not said, during the negotiations. The question of any subsequent enlargement of NATO was not discussed. Indeed, the subject was not even raised, and there was no logical way it could have been, simply because the Warsaw Pact still existed and was not dissolved until the year after. In fact, it was the existence of NATO and the continued German membership of NATO that eventually convinced the Russians that the reunification of Germany would not constitute a threat to Russian security interests because the new Germany would be tied in to a multilateral organization and not have any reason to rebuild the offensive military might of the past. When the Soviet Union collapsed in 1991, then Russian president Boris Yeltsin even flirted with the idea of a future Russian membership in NATO. Nothing indicates that Russia, at that time, considered NATO, or even a potentially larger NATO, as a threat to Russia. Nevertheless, this myth of betrayal is deeply rooted in a lot of Russian thinking.

Third, many Russians feel there has been a conspiracy. It is hard to understand, but the inner circle of the Kremlin is firmly convinced that Russia is the subject of a conspiracy, by external enemies, that aims to weaken Russia. Russian government propaganda dismissed the Rose and Orange Revolutions in Georgia and Ukraine as CIA operations that used the promotion of democracy for achieving geopolitical goals. At a minimum, this was to diminish Russian influence in the near neighborhood; at most, the goal was to use Tbilisi and Kiev as staging grounds for extending the revolutionary movement into Moscow and effecting regime change there as well. Also, according to the Russian state propaganda, the protests in Russia in the wake of Putin's reelection as president in 2012 were sponsored by the Americans. The state-controlled media identified an ever-growing list of fifth columns hostile to the state, that allegedly were also encouraged and inspired by the decadent West: homosexuals, nongovernmental organizations, activists, artists, and foreigners. Similarly, the Maidan protests in Kiev in the winter of 2013–14 were initiated and sponsored by the CIA, according to Russian propaganda. The annexation of Crimea was sold to the Russian people as a defense of ethnic Russians against neo-Nazi Ukrainians and an expansionist NATO, which allegedly would establish military bases on the peninsula. Even the decline in oil prices is seen as an American plot to weaken the Russian economy. The message is clear: Russia and the Russian way of life are under threat from hostile foreign forces, so you should rally around your leader.

In fact, the United States and Europe have done a lot to reach out to Russia and make Russia an integrated part of an inclusive Euro-Atlantic security and economy architecture. NATO and Russia adopted the Founding Act in 1997; this allowed Russia to establish a kind of embassy or permanent representation at NATO headquarters in Brussels. In 2002, the NATO-Russia Council was established. The European Union organized regular frequent summits with Russia and developed cooperation with Russia in four "common spaces": the space of economy; the space of freedom, security, and justice; the space of external security; and the space of research, education, and culture. In parallel, the United States adopted cooperation agreements with Russia, including the "strategic framework declaration" of April 2008, in which the presidents, George W. Bush and Vladimir Putin, declared, "We reaffirm that the era in which the United States and Russia considered one another an enemy or strategic threat has ended. We reject the zero-sum thinking of the Cold War, when 'what was good for Russia was bad for America' and vice versa. Rather, we are dedicated to working together, and with other nations, to address the global challenges of the 21st century, moving the U.S.-Russia relation-

ship from one of strategic competition to strategic partnership."
Nevertheless, Mr. Putin grew steadily more anti-Western, and
in August 2008, just a few months after the US-Russian declaration of partnership, he attacked neighboring Georgia.

————

SINCE THEN, THE Russian struggle with the West has increasingly become an ideological battle, with three dominant
features: Eurasianism, *"Russkiy Mir"* ("the Russian World"),
and religious orthodoxy.

Eurasianism is the idea of a unique, Russian-led civilization
that is neither European nor Asian, but should be seen as an
alternative to the Chinese civilization in the East and the
European-American civilization in the West. The idea is particularly inspired by three Russian philosophers: Ivan Ilyin, Nikolai
Berdyaev, and Vladimir Solovyov, who lived in the latter part of
the nineteenth and the first part of the twentieth centuries. All
three were looking for a uniquely Russian identity that would
allow them to cement Russia's control of its sprawling empire at
a time when it was falling behind the German, Austrian, British, and Japanese empires around its borders; all three expressed
a belief in a religious, nationalist, autocratic system. Putin often
quotes the three philosophers, and their key writings are
compulsory reading material for regional governors.

In recent times, Eurasianism has especially been promoted
by the philosopher and sociologist Alexander Dugin, who outlined the idea in several of his works, including *The Eurasian
Way as a National Idea*. In another work, *The Geopolitical Future
of Russia*, he very accurately summed up the idea that Putin has
now made into his vision:

In principle, Eurasia and our space, the heartland, Russia, remain the staging area of a new anti-bourgeois, anti-American revolution. . . . The new Eurasian empire will be constructed on the fundamental principle of the common enemy: The rejection of Atlanticism, strategic control of the U.S.A., and the refusal to allow liberal values to dominate us. This common civilizational impulse will be the basis of a political and strategic union.

The second strand is *"Russkiy Mir,"* which means "the Russian World." The idea behind this thinking is that Russian civilization goes well beyond Russia's formal borders. To promote this idea, a Russian World Foundation was established, and according to its mission statement, the Russian world is much more than the territory of the Russian Federation and the 143 million people living within its borders. The millions of ethnic Russians, native Russian-speakers, their families and dependents scattered across the globe make up the largest diaspora population the world has ever known. The *Russkiy Mir* concept is meant to reconnect the Russian diaspora with its homeland, through cultural and social programs, exchanges, and assistance in relocation.

As the third strand of its new autocracy, the Kremlin has established strong ties with the Russian Orthodox Church; indeed, Patriarch Kirill has become an integral part of the ideological mobilization. On several occasions, he supported the concept of "Great Russia," based on religious conservative nationalism. In an address at the grand opening of the Third Assembly of the Russian World in 2011, Patriarch Kirill said, "Today, too, we face a no less crucial task: Through our joint efforts, we must preserve the Russian world, dispersed in various corners of the planet, so that we do not lose the values and way of life that our forebears prized, which guided them in creating, among other things, a Great Russia."

These ideological currents gave birth to a number of concrete political initiatives. The idea of Eurasianism fed the Kremlin's political endeavors to establish the Eurasian Union, which aims at balancing China in the East with America/Europe in the West. The concept of the Eurasian Union is to create a cluster of regional states, led by Russia, that are loyal and willing to serve Moscow's interests. A key Russian goal is to make sure that Ukraine joins these structures: This would create a buffer zone between Russia and NATO. The idea of the "Russian World" and the concept of cultural influence that underpins it led to the foundation of the Kremlin's English-language television station Russia Today and the Sputnik information (or disinformation) service, and to the Putin doctrine that Russia has the right to intervene in other countries to protect what Russia perceives as the interests of Russian-speaking communities—including military intervention. And through the Church, Putin has built a springboard to influence audiences in other countries where the Eastern Orthodox Church plays a dominant role, including in the Balkans and in some EU and NATO countries. Indeed, Putin's political party has established links with conservative nationalistic parties in Europe, playing on antiliberalism, religious orthodoxy, and conservative patriotism in an attempt to create a split within NATO and the European Union. Thus, Putin's strategic goal appears to be to create a historical hybrid—a blend of the Soviet Union's superpower status with the Russian Empire's tsarist rule, built on Eurasianism, the

Russian diaspora, and the Orthodox Church. To achieve that strategic goal, the Russian leaders will primarily use three instruments: arms, energy, and a divide-and-rule approach to the West.

First, Russia is conducting a rapid military buildup, including modernizing both its nuclear and its conventional forces. Defense spending increased at an average rate of 18 percent a year from 2007 to 2014. Despite the economic difficulties caused by falling oil prices, Russia is expected to continue increasing its defense spending in the coming years and to reinforce its military presence in Central Asia, the Arctic, and the eastern part of the Mediterranean. According to the official Russian military doctrine, published in late 2014, the West, and especially NATO, is regarded as "a danger." In their larger exercises, the Russian military simulates attacks on NATO member states, including nuclear strikes. And Russia's geopolitical ambitions go beyond Europe. The Russian military intervention in Syria serves both the tactical purpose of supporting a partner, the Assad regime, and the strategic aim of ensuring Russia a seat at the table where decisions about world affairs are made.

Second, Russia has long been using the supply of energy as a weapon to subdue those neighbors that are dependent on Russian oil and gas, and thereby force them into the Russian sphere of influence through energy blackmail: low gas prices in return for supporting Russia (as in the case of Armenia), high energy prices for those who go against Russia (for example, Ukraine). At particularly tense moments, Russia has interrupted, or threatened to disconnect, the energy supply, something that has repeatedly happened to Ukraine. Ukraine gets the greater part of its oil and gas from Russia and owes

Russia's energy monopolies so much money that the debt challenges Ukraine's financial independence, and thus its real independence. In addition, Russia has consistently, and sometimes successfully, opposed the creation of alternative pipelines to Europe that would bypass the Russian monopoly and could give its neighbors more independence through larger energy supplies from the European Union.

Third, the Russian leadership is trying to weaken the cohesion of NATO because they see NATO as an obstacle to their strategic interests. Through a divide-and-rule policy of developing bilateral relations with selected NATO countries, particularly the largest, at the expense of others—in particular the former Soviet states and former Communist states in Central and Eastern Europe—they are trying to create a split, or at least a weakened unity, within NATO. Incessantly, they raise doubts about the alliance's viability and seek to weaken the alliance's role and influence in decisions on security policy. So far, NATO has maintained its unity on key issues, especially the security of those NATO members closest to Russia; but Russia's pressure is unrelenting.

These geopolitical ambitions stand in stark contrast to the weakness of the Russian economy. Indeed, Russia is a country in decline. Its current economic problems are caused by the decreasing oil prices and the Western sanctions against Russia. But more fundamentally, Russia is struggling with an outdated economy and negative demographics. Russia has a "one-crop economy," an economy that is extremely reliant on one single commodity, namely, energy, primarily oil and gas. Fuel sales accounted for more than two-thirds of Russia's export revenues in 2013, based on data from Russia's Federal Customs Service.

This overreliance on oil and gas has left the country vulnerable to fluctuations in energy prices, and the lack of diversification in the business sector has contributed to low competitiveness and poor productivity. For each hour worked, the average Russian worker contributes $26 to Russia's GDP, while the average for American workers is $67. The Russian economy is too static and lacks innovation, not least due to the low number of small and medium-sized companies. Smaller firms are the foundation of any strong and well-diversified economy. They spur innovation and respond effectively to changing times, technologies, and consumer behavior. But for years, the Kremlin has supported and protected large, state-owned companies at the expense of the small and medium-sized enterprises. Furthermore, the investment climate is extremely bad. In recent years, Russia has undertaken some economic reforms, but bureaucracy, corruption, and uncertainties about the rule of law have sent negative signals to investors, and foreign investments in Russia remain very low, while, at the same time, domestic savings are invested abroad rather than domestically. Consequently, Russia does not have access to the cutting-edge technologies its companies would need to modernize their businesses, not least the energy sector.

Overall, Russia is not a friendly country for business, domestic or foreign. This is confirmed by several international rankings. In the Transparency International Corruption Perception Index of 2015, Russia is ranked 119 out of 168 countries. In 2015, Freedom House gave the country a score of 6.75 on its corruption scale, close to the maximum corruption level of 7 for "most corrupt." Over several years, these poor scores have remained unchanged or have even deteriorated. On top of these fundamental structural economic problems, Russia suffers from negative demographics.

For decades, the population has been declining, and this trend is forecast to continue, primarily because of high mortality among men, declining birth rates, and, in general, massive health problems. Furthermore, well-educated Russians are leaving their country to seek better opportunities abroad. This falling population will remain the biggest political, economic, and social challenge for Russia in the coming decades.

While Russia is a country in decline, the Russian leadership will still have the potential to create huge geopolitical problems. In fact, historically we have seen that declining empires can be dangerous political spoilers. Think, for example, of the Ottoman Empire and the Austro-Hungarian Empire a century ago: They collapsed in the end, but they dragged the world into the abyss of World War I before they expired. A great nation in decline will fight against its waning and fight for a place in the sun. It may be willing to take the risk of military adventurism to achieve its geopolitical goals. That is how the leaders of a declining Russia are acting right now.

———

RIVAL COUNTRIES HAVE wrangled over territory in the South China Sea for centuries, but tensions have steadily increased in recent years. China lays claim to almost the whole body of water, based on a poorly defined historical claim known as the "nine-dashed line." It has backed its expansive claims with military muscle, building sunken reefs into artificial islands, siting military bases on top of them, and then saying that the existence of these "islands" gives it exclusive rights over massive areas of the surrounding sea, in violation of international norms.

This aggressive activity has pitted China against most of the other littoral states of the South China Sea. Vietnam hotly disputes China's claims; the other major claimant in the area is the Philippines, which has gone to international arbitration over China's policy. Malaysia and Brunei also lay claim to territory in the South China Sea.

In the first instance, the dispute is over territory and sovereignty over ocean areas and two island chains, the Paracels and the Spratlys, claimed in whole or in part by a number of countries in the region. Alongside the fully fledged islands, there are dozens of rocky outcrops, sandbanks, and reefs. Although largely uninhabited, the Paracels and the Spratlys may have reserves of natural resources around them. There has been little detailed exploration of the area, so estimates are largely extrapolated from the mineral wealth of neighboring areas. The sea is also a major shipping route and home to fishing grounds that supply the livelihoods of people across the region. Thus, the claim of sovereignty over these largely uninhabited rocks could have major economic implications.

But China's actions are also causing friction with the United States, which has bilateral security agreements with a number of littoral states. The United States argues that claims of exclusive rights to the sea and air space around the islands, artificial and man-made, violate the international principle of the freedom of navigation. The United States has been careful to say that its position applies to all parties, but it is widely seen as being aimed chiefly at China. Indeed, US and Australian ships and aircraft have already publicly flown and sailed across the limits that China claims as its own, arguing that such moves are an exercise of the right of freedom of navigation. So far, these moves have not been met with violence; but with the world's two greatest superpowers maneuvering so close to each other, the potential for a local flash point to become a global crisis is enormous.

———

WHILE RUSSIA IS burning the bridges to the West, President Putin has launched a "pivot" to Asia, or, more precisely, to China. Within the last few years, he has intensified contacts with China in an effort to establish a global counterweight to the United States. Chinese president Xi Jinping has received the Russian overtures politely, but the relationship between Russia and China is clearly marked by suspicion, and it is obvious that China is acting from a position of strength while Russia is acting from a position of weakness.

The political leaders in Moscow and Beijing share an authoritarian kinship that binds them together in an attempt to counterbalance American global hegemony. They detest what they perceive as a US-led, Western democratic missionary activity. In China there is a certain responsiveness to the Russian resistance to the West, its attempt to retake lost territories, and its passion for conspiracy theories. Therefore, Russia and China often act together in the UN and in other international forums to create a multipolar or bipolar world, a counterweight to the United States and its allies. Although China watched the Russian aggression against Ukraine with deep suspicion, it would also be convenient for China if Russian aggression in Europe were to distract the United States from pivoting to Asia. China is Russia's biggest trading partner and imports Russian arms and military equipment. The Chinese have been quick to exploit Russian weakness by concluding profitable agreements on gas supplies and infrastructure investments: In a desperate attempt to turn Russia's energy exports from West to East, President Putin has signed contracts with his Chinese counterpart that will ensure supplies of cheap energy to China and lucrative contracts for Chinese infrastructure builders to construct facilities including refineries and factories in Russia.

However, rivalry in Central Asia will be the greatest strategic obstacle to an alliance between Russia and China due to a gigantic project launched by the Chinese leadership. That project aims to expand China's presence in Central Asia and to strengthen its economic ties with the Middle East and Europe. More than two thousand years ago, the Chinese established a network of trade routes through Central Asia that connected China and India with the Middle East and Europe. Derived from the significant trade of silk carried out along its length, this trading network was called the Silk Road. Inspired by this ancient network of trade routes, the current Chinese leadership has launched an ambitious twenty-first-century Silk Road project. Under the motto "One Belt, One Road," China aims at creating an economic land belt that includes countries on the original Silk Road through Central Asia, West Asia, the Middle East, and Europe, as well as a maritime road that links China's port facilities with the African coast, pushing up through the Suez Canal into the Mediterranean.

The Chinese Silk Road project is a direct challenge to Russia's influence. If successful, it would give Central Asian countries alternative export markets, reducing their dependence on Russia. The Central Asian countries are in desperate need of investment capital, and as the Russian economic slow-down weakens the traditional economic ties between Russia and Central Asia, the Central Asian countries are welcoming increased Chinese investment. Trade between the Central Asian countries and China has seen explosive growth. According to IMF data, trade between China and the five post-Soviet Central Asian countries—Kazakhstan, Kyrgyzstan, Tajikistan, Turkmenistan, and Uzbekistan—increased from $1.8 billion in 2000 to $50 billion in 2013. This means that China has overtaken Russia to become the region's single largest trading partner. The Central Asia–China gas pipeline, opened in 2009, has provided the region's energy-rich economies an export route that is not controlled by Russia.

This development means that China is becoming more and more economically and politically dominant in Central Asia, a region that also plays a central role in President Putin's ambitions to create the Eurasian Union. President Xi's plans to revive the Silk Road, enhancing Chinese influence in Central Asia and strengthening Chinese economic relations with Europe, are at odds with President Putin's ambitions. China's activities in Russia's backyard will remain an obstacle to an alliance between the two countries. On the contrary, we will see toughened competition between Russia and China. Nevertheless, in light of Russia's geopolitical isolation, we will see vehement Russian efforts to develop a strategic partnership with China. Occasionally, the Russian leadership will succeed in forging ties with China when the Chinese find it opportune. But while a partnership with China is a must-have for a declining Russia, a partnership with Russia is no more than a nice-to-have, when convenient, for a rising China.

———

PRESIDENT PUTIN WANTS to be seen as a strong man. He loves the geopolitical game of major powers. He likes the direct engagement with leaders of other big countries but is not sensitive to the fate of smaller nations. On the European side, many Western European countries attach the utmost importance to a good relationship with Russia and tend to give that the highest priority. I saw that play out myself during the Danish presidency of the European Union through the second half of 2002.

The overall goal for the Danish presidency was to conclude an agreement on the enlargement of the European Union through the accession of eight Central and Eastern European countries, together with Cyprus and Malta. In that respect, we had to solve a problem related to the Russian enclave of Kaliningrad. Poland and Lithuania were among the applicant countries, and once they joined the EU, the small Russian enclave of Kaliningrad, located on the Baltic Sea, would be squeezed in between them and be surrounded by EU territory. Around a million Russian citizens would be cut off from traveling to and from Russia without a visa; in other words, Russian citizens would have to apply for a visa to travel from one part of Russia to another. Therefore, we had to find a way for Russians to get access to and from Kaliningrad through Lithuania without a visa, and we had to do it at the EU-Russia summit that I was to chair; otherwise, it would not have been possible to go on and conclude the EU's historic enlargement.

Many ideas were floated, including innovative ideas of trains whose doors would be locked during the passage over

Lithuanian territory, and high-speed trains that would not stop in Lithuania. In concrete terms, we negotiated a special transit link, a railway, through Lithuania, and the terms for using that train. The Russians were very demanding, and in fact used this issue to push for a general visa-free travel between Russia and the European Union. We feared that, in a choice between a good relationship with Russia, and Lithuania as a fully fledged member of the EU, some EU leaders would give priority to the relationship with Russia. Some of them expressed an understanding for the Russian sentiments about not being able to travel unhindered from one part of the country to another. In that big-power game, Lithuania risked being treated as a small and insignificant piece. On the other hand, Lithuania could not become a full member of the EU, including being part of the free mobility of people on the internal market, unless the problems of border controls and visas were solved.

The Lithuanian people feared that they would once again be sacrificed in the great-power game, as they had been so often during their history. A Lithuanian political magazine published a front-page illustration where a great-power corridor had cut the country in half. At one end of the corridor stood Vladimir Putin in Moscow; at the other end stood Adolf Hitler in Germany—very clear hints at the detested and felonious Nazi-Soviet Pact of the 1930s that paved the way for the Soviet annexation of the Baltic states into the Soviet Union. I was sensitive to such historical connotations, and the independence and sovereignty of the three Baltic states and their membership in NATO and the European Union had, all the way through, been one of Denmark's top foreign-policy priorities.

Leading up to the EU-Russia summit, the Russians had pursued a special negotiation strategy: Whenever they got concessions, they pocketed them and presented new demands. I decided to put a stop to that. Much to the anxiety of some camps within the EU, I was very tough with President Putin over Kaliningrad—tougher than the Russians expected, and tougher than important groups in both the European Commission and the Council of EU member states considered appropriate. I knew that Putin, a former KGB (Komitet Gosudarstvennoy Bezopasnosti; English, Committee for State Security) agent, had a reputation for being detail-minded, so I had prepared myself thoroughly, having studied both concrete negotiating texts and maps in advance. I even knew the detailed tracing of the proposed railroad, and I had prepared contingency notes for all eventualities, including how to stave off any attempts by the EU institutions to soften the hard line.

At the opening of the EU-Russia summit, I made clear that we had to find a solution at this meeting, based on the documents that were then on the table. Putin, however, demurred, and seemed ready to walk away with no deal rather than the text on the table. While the Russians had realized that the enlargement of the EU was going to become a reality, they also tried to complicate and delay the process as much as they could. Unaffected by President Putin's general demurrals, I started to go through the draft agreement paragraph by paragraph, asking him if he could clarify the Russian grievances and demands in detail. The president was clearly not prepared to dig so deeply into the details, but, assisted by his delegation, he defined eight or nine elements in the draft agreement that he considered not satisfactory. Most of them were of minor significance, so I took the chance and identified and isolated the three issues that I considered to be the most important for the Russians. I suggested giving our negotiating teams an hour to solve the outstanding issues, but added, "It is a precondition that you cannot raise new demands if these three problems are resolved," and I asked Putin, "Can you agree that this is the exhaustive list of wishes and demands, and if they are solved, there will be no new demands and we have an agreement?"

"Yes, this is the final list," Putin replied.

I said, "Okay, I think we can find a compromise on this basis." I suggested letting our negotiators go into a separate room to dive into the details while we proceeded with the other topics on the agenda.

After a little more than an hour, our negotiators came back and presented their compromise. As a result, a few very small changes were made to the text, and we concluded the EU–Russia agreement on how to solve the issue of transit to Kaliningrad. We were therefore able to remove yet another impediment to the enlargement process, but first and foremost, we had defended and protected the sovereignty of Lithuania and ensured that the country would enjoy a fully fledged membership in the European Union.

———

THIS WAS MY first political encounter with Putin, and it was a success: By paying attention to detail, and by paying attention to his own personality, I managed to achieve a historic result. Since then, I have seen him on many occasions, in both good and bad phases of his relationship with the West. Having studied the way he operates, I believe I understand how his personality influences his overall approach to other countries and his negotiation tactics. Based on that, I strongly recommend three strategies in dealing with President Putin and the Russian leadership.

First, it is of utmost importance to keep unity within the Western organizations, notably NATO and the European Union. Putin loves to play one nation or group of nations off against others, thereby weakening his counterparts. When he realizes that he is up against a strong, united front, it is easier to get him to engage constructively.

Second, it is crucial to demonstrate firmness. Putin is a straight talker himself, and as much as he likes to cultivate his strongman image, he also respects firmness and clear talk when he meets it. Indulgence and appeasement are considered weaknesses he can exploit.

Third, it is imperative to negotiate from a position of strength. Putin respects power above all else. If he realizes that he is dealing with invincible Western economic, political, and military strength, he will more easily appreciate the need for cooperation rather than confrontation. The tragic reality is that Putin has to be made to appreciate that need, because he cannot, or will not, see it himself. Russia's current leaders seem not to want an open Russian society living in peace with their neighbors and the world; instead, they seem to want a closed and defensive society based on the chauvinist myth that Russia has the right to dominate a special sphere of interest, and anyone who disagrees is an enemy. It is that mentality that led Russia to support breakaway regions in Georgia and Moldova, to violate Ukraine's sovereignty and territorial integrity, to breach Russia's international commitments, and to annex Crimea at gunpoint through a so-called referendum that was illegal and illegitimate.

The Russian attack on Ukraine was the biggest disappointment of my five-year mandate as secretary-general of NATO because, fundamentally, I think that Russia and the West have a shared interest in cooperation and partnership. We are very much dependent on each other, and we in the West have made enormous efforts to build a constructive relationship. Economically, the European Union is Russia's number one trading partner, accounting for more than 40 percent of all trade. EU countries get most of their energy imports from Russia. European countries import more than 80 percent of Russia's oil exports and about 75 percent of its natural gas exports. Nor is this just about Europe: The United States imports about 5 percent of Russian oil, and it is the leading investor in Russia, followed by Germany and France. All in all, Europe and North America represent approximately 90 percent of the foreign investments in Russia, and the bulk of Russian investments abroad have Europe and North America as the destination. So economically speaking, partnership means profit: The more Russia and the West work together, the more we earn together.

And the same goes for security. Economic cooperation brings economic benefits; security cooperation brings security benefits. A genuine partnership between Russia and NATO would improve Euro-Atlantic security. Our allies would be reassured that they had nothing to fear from the east, and Russia could focus its limited resources on real threats from the south, including the North Caucasus. Russia has, like Western countries, suffered from terrorism, some of it homegrown. We have a strong, mutual interest in combating terrorism. That is why, since the end of the Cold War, we in the West have put a huge amount of effort into developing a partnership with Russia.

I am often asked, "Wasn't that a bit naive? Wasn't the idea that Russia really wanted a partnership with NATO and the EU just a dream?" My answer is: "We were not dreamers. We gave it a try with open eyes." And I still think we did the right thing. After the end of the Cold War we had a generational duty to strive for a better future; to create a Europe whole, free, and at peace for the sake of future generations. It was the smart thing to do and the right thing to do, and that's why I am deeply disappointed by Russia's actions, because those actions show that Russia's current leaders do not share our vision.

But just as our eyes were open when we launched the NATO-Russia Council, we have to keep them open now; and if we look at Russia's actions with open eyes, we can see what could be called "twenty-first-century revisionism": attempts to turn back the clock, draw new dividing lines on our maps, subdue populations, rewrite the international rule book, and use force to solve problems, rather than the international mechanisms that we have spent decades building. This is happening today in the heart of Europe. It is a wake-up call for all of us. We had thought that such behavior had been consigned to history, but it is back. It is dangerous. And only the united power of the democracies of the world, led by the United States, will be strong enough to preserve the global order and consign such behavior, once more, to history.

CHAPTER 8

AN ALLIANCE FOR DEMOCRACY

The price of liberty is eternal vigilance.
—THOMAS JEFFERSON

The best hope for peace in our world is the expansion
of freedom in all the world.
—GEORGE W. BUSH

On the evening of November 9, 1989, I was sitting in my office in the Ministry of Taxation in Copenhagen. Appointed minister as a thirty-four-year-old in 1987, I was the youngest member of the cabinet, and very determined to demonstrate skills and efficiency that could compensate for my youth. I worked day and night, and very often I spent the evenings in my office, reading and managing files; I let my staff go off duty to make sure I was not disturbed. That Thursday evening, too, I had intended to spend some exciting time with my tax files. However, it was hard to concentrate. Historic events were unfolding not far from Copenhagen, in Berlin. I zapped around the television channels, and they were all broadcasting live from East Berlin, where people had started crossing the wall between East and West Berlin. There were incredible pictures of people standing on top of the Wall; jumping into West Berlin; opening the border gates and crossing the formerly heavily guarded checkpoints—for most easterners, the first time they visited West Berlin; images of happy people partying in the streets. In the end, I surrendered to television. I could not *not* watch that moment of history being made, and of freedom breaking free. The discrepancy between the historic events in Berlin and the loneliness of my ministerial office was simply too great for me to keep my attention on the technicalities of the Danish value-added tax (VAT) system.

During my upbringing in school and elsewhere, we had not learned much about the people, the countries, and the way of life behind the Iron Curtain. We simply did not know much about the East. It was a closed land, dark and gray, and most of us who grew up in the shadow of the Wall and the Iron Curtain could not imagine that change could happen, or at least that it could happen so fast. President Reagan had called on Gorbachev to tear down the Wall, but now Berliners took the matter into their own hands; and with the Wall, Communism also fell, and the moral, economic, and political bankruptcy of that inhuman ideology was declared.

People in the former Communist states threw off the yoke of dictatorship and started determinedly on the journey toward freedom and democracy. A new era began, in which the peoples of Europe turned their backs on the Cold War and opened a new chapter with the aim of creating a new Europe, whole, free, and at peace. People's strong will to be free had prevailed over oppression. Optimism flourished, and everyone was convinced that the superiority of liberal democracy would triumph over autocracy all over the world.

I saw that will to freedom displayed twenty-two years later under quite different circumstances. My house in Copenhagen is full of mementos from my years in government and service, but I find my eye wandering to a scarf I was given by a young freedom fighter in Libya in 2011. For me, it is a reminder of the universal yearning for freedom. I was the secretary-general of NATO at the time. We were visiting Tripoli on October 31, the last day of our mission, Operation Unified Protector. As we drove down the streets of the capital, we could see graffiti sprayed on the walls: "Thank you NATO."

At a reception for young freedom fighters, one young man stepped forward and gifted me the scarf, which was festooned with revolutionary colors. Over the course of the afternoon, the fighters spoke of a freedom that they had never known under Colonel Gadhafi: their desire for a society free of tribal and religious strife, the freedom to choose, the freedom to pursue dreams. They dreamed about peace, progress, and prosperity. I was moved by their dreams and inspired by their gift. It was given in gratitude for aiding their liberation, but I also thought of it as a down payment on the future of a free Libya.

———

IN 1993, I READ Francis Fukuyama's book *The End of History and the Last Man* with great interest, and as a classical European liberal I took great pleasure in his prediction of the inevitable triumph of liberal capitalist democracy. As he famously put it, "At the end of history, there are no serious ideological competitors left to liberal democracy," and in the spirit of the optimism that dominated after the end of the Cold War, he elaborated further: "What we may be witnessing is not just the end of the Cold War or the passing of a particular period of post-war history, but the end of history as such: That is, the end point of mankind's ideological evolution, and the universalization of Western liberal democracy as the final form of human government."

Encouraged by the fall of the Wall, the collapse of the Soviet Union, and the beginning opening of China, I concurred with Fukuyama's analysis. I firmly believed that capitalism and liberal democracy would go from strength to strength over the world, simply because it was demonstrably the most successful model for the development of a society, and from that would also flow a new world order, as outlined by President George H. W. Bush in his address to a joint session of Congress, "Toward a New World Order," on September 11, 1990. In that speech, he set out his vision of a new world, where "the rule of law supplants the rule of the jungle" and where nations "recognize the shared responsibility for freedom and justice." Liberal capitalism and democracy had won the battle of ideas.

It turned out to be a brief period of hope: In time, we learned the hard way that there was no universal agreement on the unparalleled strength of liberal capitalism and democracy. In my many meetings with the highly experienced and cunning Russian foreign minister Sergey Lavrov, for example, he often spoke about the need for a multipolar world and the competition between different value systems and ideas, implicitly confirming that liberal democracy would find it hard to get past the watchdogs of the Kremlin. Indeed, President Putin spoke warmly about "sovereign democracy," which, I understood, was a very particular Russian sort of "managed democracy" necessitated by the complexity of Russian society. "Managed democracy" is a contradiction in terms: It is, in fact, undemocratic, since it means that power is not actually vested in the people but their managers. In reality, Russia has moved from an admittedly somewhat chaotic democracy in the 1990s to an admittedly more orderly autocracy. Furthermore, a resurgent Russia has challenged the rules-based international order by taking land by force from Ukraine and by violating Ukraine's sovereignty through active support for separatists in eastern Ukraine. Autocracy has made a comeback.

In the Middle East and North Africa, too, we have seen autocrats striking back. Against the backdrop of victory, joy, and optimism among the young freedom fighters in Tripoli, it has been depressing to see the democratic forces sidelined and Libya plunging into chaos and becoming a breeding ground for extremism and terrorism. It has been disappointing to witness the failure of democracy in Egypt and heartbreaking to witness the brutal crackdown on freedom activists by the Syrian regime. What started as an Arab Spring has turned into an icy winter.

And overall, we are seeing a global decline in political rights and civil liberties. In 2016, for the tenth consecutive year, *Freedom in the World*, Freedom House's annual report on the condition of global political rights and civil liberties, showed an overall decline. The acceptance of democracy as the world's dominant form of government is, according to the organization, under greater threat than at any point in the last twenty-five years. This pattern held true across geographical regions, with more declines than gains in the Middle East and North Africa, Eurasia, sub-Saharan Africa, Europe, and the Americas, and an even split in Asia Pacific. A troubling number of large, economically powerful, or regionally influential countries moved backward: Russia, Venezuela, Egypt,

Turkey, Thailand, Kenya, and Azerbaijan. The worst reversals affected freedom of expression, civil society, and the rule of law. We must realize that liberal capitalism and democracy are not unchallenged systems. They cannot be taken for granted: Autocrats will do all they can to remain autocrats, and together, they have a shared interest in challenging the liberal world order and the ideas of individual liberty, free-market economy, and the rule of law. As far back as 2008, Robert Kagan concluded that autocracy is coming back, and, as a polemic response to Fukuyama, he stated that we are witnessing "the return of history and the end of dreams."

It may well be that we are witnessing the return of history, but I refuse to put an end to dreams. We can be proud of what our free societies have achieved, and I insist on keeping alive the dream that liberal democracy will prevail over autocracy and oppression, so I prefer to speak about "the return of the history and the continuation of dreams."

————

PERHAPS THE BIGGEST threat to the dream of universal liberal democracy comes from deep within liberal democracy itself. The world's liberal democracies are vastly superior to the world's autocracies by almost every measure except one: the will to lead. Autocratic leaders do not second-guess themselves; democratic societies by nature tend to second-guess themselves. One could even take this argument one step further: The more successful and prosperous democratic societies become, the more time they spend ripping themselves apart politically, undermining their own will to lead on the international stage.

At the beginning of the nineteenth century, Alexis de

Tocqueville observed a certain optimism in American society. The Americans "have all a lively faith in the perfectibility of man. . . . They all consider society as a body in a state of improvement." Political and social observers have echoed this sentiment and spirit of optimism for centuries as an essential feature of not just the American dream but also of the social and economic institutions of American civil society.

Today, when the United States has never been more powerful, prosperous, and protective of minority rights, the public mood is much gloomier. A Pew Research study from 2015 shows that Americans are not highly confident in the nation's future. Fewer than half (45 percent) expressed quite a lot of confidence in the future of the United States. Just 19 percent of those under thirty say that the United States stands above other nations. Confidence in the future of the United States is lower today than it was in the mid-1970s: For example, a 1975 survey by Gallup found that 60 percent had quite a lot of confidence in the future of the United States. That has fallen to 45 percent now.

Another poll from 2015, commissioned for the *Atlantic* and the Aspen Institute, points out that a majority of Americans (75 percent) believe that the American dream is suffering, that obstacles to realizing the dream are "more severe today than ever" (69 percent), and that, overall, the nation is on the wrong track (64 percent).

Self-doubt is not a model for success. Americans need to recall that they have made stunning progress, creating the world's first mass-prosperity society and the world's most powerful magnet for ambitious immigrants. The United States alone has a universal appeal, and many people want to be

American. US presidential elections are watched with passion in the world, not least because of the soft-power credentials of the United States. Americans need to rediscover their pride in being American.

Western societies are more democratic, more liberal, and more protective of minority rights than any societies seen in previous times—indeed, they are a strong model for success and individual happiness. There is a need for the next US president to inspire optimism and hope; we need to see a show-down with the self-doubt, sometimes even self-hatred, that characterizes much of the public debate in the United States and other free societies.

Many leftists like to blame the West and free liberal democracy and capitalism for all the problems in the world. Terrorism? Caused by Western oppression of minorities. African kleptocracy? Caused by the legacy of Western colonialism. Hunger and poverty? Caused by Western capitalism. Autocracy and tyranny? Caused by Western imperialism. We know the entire arsenal of accusations. Western culture and the Western way of life seem to be the mother of all of the world's problems.

It is tempting to dismiss these arguments as the thoughts of a few die-hard, unreformed Communists, but Western self-doubt unfortunately extends far beyond the community of hard-core leftists. In academia in particular, it has become commonplace to focus on the shortfalls of Western history and culture rather than the greatness of Western civilization. American and European universities used to require deep immersion in the classics of Western philosophy. Today, this solid philosophical grounding has been replaced with a focus on pure technical training or, even worse, outright rejection of Western values and civilization. Allan Bloom described this development well in his 1987 classic, *The Closing of the American Mind*, and the situation has hardly improved in the three decades since then.

The lack of a solid appreciation for the Western roots of liberal democracy among academically educated elites in politics, business, and culture leads to an instinctive moral relativism that undermines the will to lead. Too often, political correctness blocks out moral clarity and gets in the way of sound decision making.

In my view, one of the key weaknesses of the Obama presidency has been the administration's inclination toward moral and cultural relativism. President Obama's speech at the National Prayer Breakfast in February 2015 was a prime example of this relativism. Speaking of religious violence around the world and in the context of the brutal rise of IS in Syria, the president was quick to point out Western shortcomings:

> And lest we get on our high horse and think this is unique to some other place, remember that during the Crusades and the Inquisition, people committed terrible deeds in the name of Christ. In our home country, slavery and Jim Crow all too often was justified in the name of Christ. . . . So this is not unique to one group or one religion. There is a tendency in us, a sinful tendency that can pervert and distort our faith.

Another example was President Obama's speech in Havana, Cuba, on March 22, 2016, comparing Communist movements to the American Revolution in 1776:

The ideals that are the starting point for every revolution—America's revolution, Cuba's revolution, the liberation movements around the world—those ideals find their truest expression, I believe, in democracy.

I agree with President Obama that all religions fall short, all revolutions have some elements of nobility, and all human beings have sinful tendencies. But it is equally true that some religions have more shortcomings than others, some revolutions are nobler than others, and some human beings are more sinful than others. It is only when we are willing to say openly that some actions and some ways of life are better than others that we can move the human race forward.

To a certain extent, self-flogging and self-laceration reflect one of the virtues of Western culture: The inbuilt pressure of criticism pushes us to question established truths and seek new knowledge and cognition, which in turn paves the way for renewal and progress. Yet very often, the criticism is not a way of refining and improving the real achievements of Western culture, not least of which is the freedom to criticize. Denunciation seems to be relished out of a cultural relativism that builds on the premise that all values and principles are of equal quality, and it does not acknowledge the exceptional strength of individual liberty, liberal democracy, capitalism, and the rule of law.

The time has come for a showdown with this tyranny of guilt. The fact is that Western culture has brought great progress to the world. The Enlightenment brought a new understanding of faith and science, which paved the way for knowledge, progress, and individual freedom. Liberal democracy gave people the opportunity to get rid of tyranny and despotism and guaranteed certain rights for the individual. Liberal capitalism and globalization have brought prosperity and moved hundreds of millions of people out of poverty and hunger.

We can be proud of these achievements. Instead of self-doubt, we need self-confidence. Instead of denunciation, we need recognition. Instead of Western masochism, we need Western uplift. As leader of the free world, the American president must emanate and enunciate a clear conviction in the supremacy of Western liberalism and capitalism, and stimulate self-confidence, instill trust in the future, and raise optimism and hope for all the people in the world who are yearning for liberty.

———

SELF-DOUBT AND DISCORD among the world's democracies are major weaknesses that autocracies often seek to exacerbate and exploit for their own purposes. During the Cold War, the Soviet Union actively supported the Western European peace and environmental movements in an effort to divide the United States and Europe and to undermine NATO's nuclear deterrent. Communist bloc propaganda actively nurtured the view that Western capitalism led to the oppression of the poor, the sick, and minorities. In more recent years, autocracies like Russia, China, and Iran have actively continued this combination of geopolitical positioning and political propaganda to undermine liberal democratic unity. Nowhere is this effort by the autocracies to undermine the will of the democracies more evident than at the United Nations.

The United Nations began as a noble expression of liberal democratic universalism. The United Nations Universal Declaration of Human Rights states very clearly: "All human beings are born free and equal in dignity and rights," and "everyone has the right to life, liberty and security of person." Sadly, the UN's role and credibility as guardian of universal human rights has been dramatically undermined by the creation of a Human Rights Council whose members include several autocratic states that suppress human rights at home and refuse to recognize the universality of human rights abroad. This is all the more devastating because the original idea of the creation of the United Nations and the adoption of the Declaration of Human Rights was precisely to affirm the universality of man's basic freedoms. For the UN itself to have been muzzled by the forces of oppression is a tragedy.

Furthermore, the aura of democratic legitimacy that still surrounds the United Nations has time and time again been used by autocracies to block democracies from taking action on the international stage to combat genocide and tyranny and to promote liberal democracy. In most liberal democracies, it is important politically to secure a UN mandate before engaging in military action. By assigning such importance to the UN, we effectively give autocracies like China and Russia the ability to paralyze the United States and its democratic allies through their veto power on the UN Security Council.

The United Nations started out as a noble effort and a useful geopolitical tool for exercising American global leadership. Unfortunately, the UN has now become the geopolitical expression of moral relativism, all too often refusing to distinguish between good and evil, preventing decisive action on the global stage when it is most needed. However, it is also important to recognize that the United States needs an institution like the United Nations that will allow the American president to mobilize the world's democracies in a united front the same way that Harry Truman did in the Korean War and George H. W. Bush did in the First Gulf War.

The United States is indispensable in its ability to protect and promote freedom and to prevent conflicts, to resolve conflicts, and to help with post-conflict reconstruction. However, the United States should not be left to carry out that job alone: Smart American leadership should strive for alliance-building. While the United States, due to its strength, could carry out most of the tasks alone, it would gain more legitimacy, greater political strength, and additional resources by bringing in like-minded allies and partners to help do the job. Furthermore, there is a need to create an overwhelming, credible, and strong liberal democratic supremacy in order to counterbalance the rising and assertive autocracies. Today, the United States cooperates with other democracies in many different contexts: globally, for example, in the G7 (that is, Canada, France, Germany, Italy, Japan, the UK, and the United States); regionally, for example, in NATO; or bilaterally, for example, in the US-Japan defense pact. But there is no single forum for the world's democracies to meet and discuss issues of common interest, and possibly coordinate policies in the United Nations and other international organizations.

To create a stronger global liberal democratic community, the next American president should use his or her power to convene the world's liberal democracies in a strong "Alliance for Democracy." Such an alliance would bring together nations from around the world whose common characteristic would be that they are democracies. And precisely that would be the alliance's main strength: It would create a community of the world's free societies; a community that is not based on size, regional location, producer interests, or stage of economic development. It would be a community of shared values, individual liberty, economic freedom, democracy, and the rule of law; a community that would bolster the identity and potency of democracy in a world where the forces of oppression are trying to regain ground.

The Alliance for Democracy would consist of a diverse group of countries from around the globe, small and large, rich and poor, strong and weak, and both old and new democracies. Overall, the objective of the alliance would be to create a forum where the world's democracies could meet on a regular basis to discuss global issues, coordinate their policies, and possibly take joint action to reinforce liberal democratic values around the world. It would be a political alliance between governments, rather than a cumbersome bureaucracy: The heads of state and government should meet at least once a year, while more frequent meetings should be held at the ministerial level, as needed and as appropriate.

In more concrete terms, the Alliance for Democracy could conceivably have five tasks. First, it could help confront common security challenges, including terrorism. The democracies could enhance their intelligence cooperation to find out where the terrorists are, strengthen financial cooperation to locate the terrorists' sources of financing, dry those sources up and block them, and improve law enforcement and judicial cooperation to apprehend them, try them, and jail them.

Second, it could work to make the liberal capitalist democracies more prosperous, competitive, and attractive by promoting commerce, economic growth, and job creation. The alliance could strive to be an attractive trading area. By reducing tariffs and other trade barriers, by promoting investments, and by granting members of the alliance a privileged status for the transfer of new technology, the Alliance for Democracy would bolster its position in relation to the world's autocracies and would create strong incentives for the autocracies to become democracies.

Liberal capitalism is the most efficient model to further prosperity, meet people's needs, and eradicate poverty. The liberalization of trade and investment opens up new opportunities for millions of people throughout the world, bringing us all closer together. The free market gives consumers the power to ensure that what they want is what is actually produced. Free trade ensures a global distribution of labor that provides us with a maximum variety of goods and services at the lowest possible price. Free mobility of labor and capital ensures the most efficient use of resources. And vitally, if we allow developing countries free access to the world market, they can combat poverty on their own terms.

I firmly believe that free trade helps to promote peace by strengthening the economic ties between peoples and countries. As the French economist Frédéric Bastiat once put it, "When goods do not cross borders, soldiers will." Without any doubt, the protectionism of the 1930s contributed to the rise of Nazism and the subsequent war. Free markets, free mobility, free trade: all prerequisites for growth, prosperity, and progress—and peace.

Third, the Alliance for Democracy could help promote democracy directly, through advice, support, and assistance. Based on members' different experiences in developing democracy, the alliance and its individual members could help new and emerging democracies build the necessary strong and stable democratic institutions, strengthen civil society, and generally develop democratic culture and thinking.

In particular, the alliance could seek to advance free speech, which is the most precious civic right we have and which has come under threat in recent years from violent extremists as well as our own internal political correctness. Free speech is the safeguard for all other freedoms. Without the freedom to discuss all matters, there can be no true democracy. The freedom to speak against those in power is our bulwark against tyranny. The freedom to pose critical questions about established truth and dogmas is the only way to ensure progress, renewal, and development.

Fourth, the alliance could be a forum for the coordination of policies in other international organizations. The alliance would not replace or substitute for other international organizations such as the UN or the Group of Twenty (G20, comprising nineteen countries plus the European Union). There is a continued need for international forums where the countries of the world come together regardless of their form of government. In the UN, autocratic and democratic countries meet to discuss global challenges. Sometimes it proves impossible to reach an agreement; sometimes they manage to find a compromise. There is a need for such international forums, but it is equally important for the world's democracies to have a forum where they can coordinate their policies in the UN and other international organizations—not least, so that they could push for reforms to make the UN more effective.

Fifth, the Alliance for Democracy could also be used for joint action, particularly humanitarian interventions. This is a very sensitive theme, but sometimes intervention is needed to uphold the basic principles of the UN Charter, including the protection of human rights. As a general rule, this should be based on an authorization from the UN Security Council, but too often it is difficult to reach agreement on such mandates. The Alliance for Democracy could use its muscle to push, persuade, and cajole members of the Security Council. In extreme cases, action may even be necessary without an explicit mandate from the UN Security Council. An example could be an unscrupulous dictator who uses chemical weapons against his own population. The use of chemical weapons is strictly prohibited under international law, and should be sanctioned immediately, possibly with a military strike. It increases the legitimacy of such an action if the world's democracies work together.

Who would have the opportunity to join the Alliance for Democracy? A key condition for membership would, of course, be to hold regular free and fair elections, but this would only be the start. Democracy is more than just holding elections. A true democracy also guarantees the protection of individual rights. Citizens of an alliance member state should enjoy both fundamental political rights, including the right to vote, stand for election, and participate in government, and fundamental civic rights, including freedom of expression, freedom of assembly, and freedom of religion. These rights must be guaranteed by the rule of law. According to Freedom House's *Freedom in the World 2016 Report*, eighty-six countries can be assessed as "free." This is the sort of assessment that could lead to consideration for membership. Countries that do not meet the membership criteria for the time being would, over time, have the chance to join the alliance when they fulfill the necessary criteria. Indeed, one of the aims of the alliance is precisely to increase the incentives for non-democracies to embrace democratic principles, values, and practices. In Europe, the EU and NATO served this function by defining the conditions and criteria for membership that candidates had to meet in order to become members of the organizations; a similar incentive given to countries from beyond Europe should have a similar effect.

Of course, there is no guarantee that the world's democracies will agree on everything, but that objection can be used against any international organization. The UN is frequently in disagreement; so is the G20. The criterion for membership in the G20 is the size of a country's economy, not a set of shared values. The Alliance for Democracy would be composed of countries that share common democratic values and have democratically elected governments with popular legitimacy. The probability of them bridging their differences and generating effective cooperation would be greater than in organizations that also include autocratic governments. But the purpose, content, and composition of the alliance would be so attractive that members would undoubtedly do their utmost to ensure a strong unity, and if the American president executes a strong and determined leadership, most democracies would readily rally around the world's strongest democracy.

As the world's largest market-oriented democracy, India will be one of the main pillars in an Alliance for Democracy.

India is a fast-rising economy and has a vital interest in upholding a rules-based international order that provides an efficient and reliable framework for trade, investments, and economic cooperation. In that respect, India shares interests with other democracies in securing the "global commons," such as free and open sea-lanes, safe trade routes, free information and communication lines, and an open, secure, and reliable cyberspace, through enhanced maritime security and cybersecurity. Strategically located at the heart of the Indo-Pacific region, India also has a key interest in working with like-minded countries to ensure that maritime and territorial disputes are settled amicably according to the rule of international law, and that China, in particular, does not bend international rules to suit itself. While India, the United States, and other democracies want to engage China economically and on issues such as climate change, terrorism, and nuclear proliferation, none are willing to see China dominate the critical sea-lanes of the Indian Ocean and South China Sea, through which a major share of the world's energy and container traffic is shipped.

———

THE ESTABLISHMENT OF the Alliance for Democracy would not rule out cooperation with autocratic governments. Members of the Alliance for Democracy could continue to do business with and have political interaction with, for example, China and Russia. Obviously, autocratic governments can be expected to distance themselves from the formation of the Alliance for Democracy and to criticize it—it is, after all, created to counterbalance autocracy. But experience shows that, in the long run, it creates more respect and relaxation and stability if the free world negotiates from a position of unity and strength.

In the somewhat hyped discussion on China surpassing the United States as the world's biggest economy, we should not forget that being the biggest is not necessarily equivalent to being the strongest. Harvard University professor Joseph S. Nye has made the case for continued American supremacy convincingly in his book *Is the American Century Over?* While China will become the world's largest economy within a few years' time, the United States will still remain the world's strongest power, and that will not change anytime soon, if ever. The average income per capita in China is only 20 percent of the average per capita income in the United States; when you multiply 20 percent of the American income by 1.3 billion people, it adds up to an economy that is huge, but not necessarily deep. When it comes to the strength, competitiveness, dynamism, and attractiveness of economic systems, the United States is by far the strongest nation in the world, and it will take a wide span of years for China to catch up, if ever. And while China has increased its military spending enormously during recent years, the United States is by far the strongest military power in the world, representing 34 percent of global defense investment, compared to China's 12 percent. And when it comes to the stock of accumulated modern military capabilities, the discrepancy is even more pronounced.

China's leaders know these realities very well. That is why their preferred option appears at present to be to work within the rules-based international order in constructive cooperation with the United States. China and the United States will be competitors, yes, but as a rising state, China would rather work practically to reshape rules and institutions within the system than confront and undercut the system. Consequently, the United States and its allies should pursue a balanced approach toward China, with equal engagement, deterrence, and incentives. The mere existence of the Alliance for Democracy would be a kind of hedge, as it would signal that China should not play games with democracies in her neighborhood. And it would increase the chances for constructive cooperation with China as the Chinese leadership realizes the overwhelming supremacy of the world's democracies and appreciates the benefits of productive collaboration.

The Alliance for Democracy could engage in frequent meetings with China to build confidence and trust. There might be room for cooperation in areas where interests are congruent with China's, including the fight against terrorism, regional stabilization, regional security in and around Afghanistan, counter-piracy, climate change and pollution, stabilizing the global economy, and promoting global economic growth. It is also important to engage China in countering the proliferation of weapons of mass destruction.

And it would be essential to address cyber crime and the alleged Chinese involvement in hacking and spying against businesses and government institutions in other countries. The democracies of the world must make clear that this behavior cannot, and will not, be tolerated. In parallel, the United States should reinforce its defense cooperation with countries in the Asia Pacific region to deter China from further muscle-flexing in the South China and East China Seas. But that deterrence should be accompanied by strong incentives for China to work peacefully and positively within the multilateral rules-based international system. The emergence of a major Asia Pacific trade integration program, the Trans-Pacific Partnership (TPP), in which China does not participate, and a major multilateral financial institution, the Asian Infrastructure Investment Bank, in which the United States does not participate, are strategic failures. While China must respect the fundamental principles of the international rule of law, her participation in multilateral efforts should be encouraged, not restrained. When the time is ripe, the participants in the TPP agreement should consider inviting China to participate, and within the global economic institutions, China and other emerging powers should be assigned voting weights that reflect their growing prominence in the world economy.

———

WE NEED FRESH, new thinking on the theories and political practices of the global and regional balance of power. Traditionally, the discussion has been dominated by the question of whether the world is, or should be, unipolar, bipolar, or multipolar. In a unipolar world, there is one dominant power; in a bipolar world, there are two dominant powers that balance each other; and in a multipolar world, there are several centers of power that balance one another. Implicitly, the bi- and multipolar power balances build on a static world where the status quo is a prerequisite for stability. But in today's and tomorrow's world of cross-border information technology, this fixed status quo is not a realistic approach, and neither is it desirable if we want to protect and promote freedom and democracy. Consequently, our attitudes toward the concept of balance of power need to be revised.

I recognize that the balance of power has worked before in history. One oft-cited example is the 1648 Treaty of Westphalia, which brought an end to the Thirty Years' War in Europe and established a balance of power that prevented major conflicts between the dominant European countries. Similarly, it is often stated that the 1815 Congress of Vienna, which ended the Napoleonic Wars, created a new balance of power that prevented major wars for the next hundred years, until the outbreak of the First World War. So it may well be that the theory of international balances between major powers worked in the age of Westphalia, in the seventeenth century, and the Congress of Vienna, in the nineteenth century. But not in today's globalized world. Today, transnational forces play a much stronger role, challenging the power balance and weakening nation-states within the delicately calibrated system: Just think of IS, and how it is trying to redraw the borders of the Middle East.

But more important, the information revolution has created drastically changed conditions for international politics. Thanks to satellite TV, the Internet, and social media, people all over the world can follow developments and events in other parts of the world in real time. People in autocratic countries can see with their own eyes the freedom and better life opportunities in free Western societies. They want the same and demand to get rid of autocracy, repression, corruption, and kleptocracy. The autocrats can no longer sustain their oppressive regimes by keeping their people ignorant of conditions outside. In the long run, repression leads to rebellion: just think of the Arab Spring.

In parallel, people in free societies can watch and follow in real life and real time the horrors and cruelty of brutal regime clampdowns and despicable terrorist acts. This, in turn, may lead to popular demands for action against the perpetrators, even if no vital national security interests are at stake. Just think of Gadhafi's threat to exterminate the population of Benghazi in the winter of 2011: In Europe, even traditionally pacifist leftist groups supported military action against the Gadhafi regime—with their own eyes they could see the evil building up, right on Europe's doorstep.

The problem with the theory of power balance is that it builds on the belief that maintaining the status quo should be the main objective for foreign policy, but people will not accept the status quo. Ukraine and Georgia are a good example: They want to leave the Russian sphere of interest and join the democratic Euro-Atlantic institutions, and of course that will disturb the power balance in Europe. Writing in the magazine *Foreign Policy* on these countries' aspirations and the tensions they have caused with Russia, Professor Stephen Walt argues: "The solution to this crisis is for the United States and its allies to abandon the dangerous and unnecessary goal of endless NATO expansion and do whatever it takes to convince Russia that we want Ukraine to be a neutral buffer state in perpetuity."

That is just not how free societies should work. How can we deny the peoples of Ukraine and Georgia their inherent right to decide their future themselves? Ukrainians and Georgians are not second-class citizens: They deserve the same chances that so many other peoples have won over the years, and it is in contradiction to the fundamental liberal democratic principles to suggest otherwise. And the Ukrainians and Georgians will not sit down tamely and allow the great powers to draw a new dividing line across Europe, with them on the wrong side of the line. They will come out on the streets in their hundreds of thousands, as they have done so often in the past, and who among us will dare to tell them that they should shut up and go home?

In today's world, the status quo and the static nature of the power balance will not create stability: They will merely repress the pressure for change until it explodes. So the theories of regional power balance and spheres of interest are outdated and won't work in the globalized information society. Professor Walt is a prominent representative of the "realist" school of foreign policy. The theory of realism suggests that the United States should not intervene in international conflicts unless existential national interests are at stake. In *Foreign Affairs* in 2005, Professor Walt argued that the United States should pursue a strategy of "offshore balancing": "This strategy assumes that only a few parts of the world are of strategic importance to the United States, such as Europe, industrialized Asia and the Persian Gulf. Instead of controlling these areas directly, the United States would rely on local actors to maintain the regional balance of power."

I'm afraid that the theory of "offshore balancing," with its idea that the United States can rely on local actors to maintain the balance of power, does not work in practice. Consider Europe. The dominant geostrategic challenge of the continent is the balance between Russia and Europe. The key question is: How do we secure a Europe that is whole, free, and at peace? For many of the Central and Eastern European countries, which only recently emerged from half a century of totalitarian domination imposed by Moscow, this translates into an existential question about a credible defense against possible Russian aggression.

Can the Europeans solve this task on their own? The short and candid answer is no. First, the Europeans don't have the necessary military strength. In terms of both conventional and nuclear forces, Russia is far stronger than Europe. Certainly, the Europeans' combined investments in defense represent about 15 percent of total global military spending, while Russia's military investments represent only about 5 percent of the global total. However, the European defense investments are not effective, and the defense is fragmented: more than thirty-five different national armies with independent, sovereign decision-making mechanisms. Overall, the European military is too static, too slow to mobilize, and too limited in its capacity to deploy; it is poorly developed technologically; and the total firepower is too limited.

Next, could the Europeans develop a common defense or integrate their defense better, for example, in the EU? In theory yes, but in practice no. Indeed, there have been attempts to develop a common defense dimension of the EU. But it is a paper tiger. France is traditionally at the forefront of efforts to develop a common EU defense policy, sometimes at the expense of NATO. But at the same time, it is France that strongly insists on maintaining national sovereignty over defense. And that is the fundamental obstacle to developing a common European army: Europe remains a continent of independent, sovereign nation-states. And national sovereignty is inextricably linked to national defenses with national political sovereignty. Therefore, we will not see a European army, either in my lifetime or my children's or grandchildren's. Perhaps we will see a stronger defense dimension within the EU, but the real operational capability will remain extremely limited. The real

defense business will still have to take place through NATO—
that is, with a strong American involvement.

The Americans have rightfully requested that European
allies invest more in defense to ensure a fairer burden sharing within the alliance. But even if Europe invested more in
her own defense, Europeans would not be able to counter the
increasingly assertive Russia. Fundamentally, there is a lack of
political cohesion in the approach to Russia and a lack of political will to use military force. The three biggest military powers
in Europe are the UK, France, and Germany. But they have
very different approaches to Russia and to the use of robust
military force. For historical reasons, Germany is reluctant to
use military force, and is hesitant to challenge Russia; it is more
inclined to seek rapprochement and appeasement. France and
the UK are much more willing to use force if necessary, but
they are very different in their approach to Russia. While the
UK insists on a robust rejection of Russia's ambitions to re-
establish a Russian sphere of interest in Eastern Europe, the
French political leaders, across the political spectrum, are far
more accommodating to Russia.

These fundamental differences among Europe's big countries
create a lot of anxiety about security, in particular in the Central and Eastern European countries. Throughout history,
they have been traded among different empires, with no
regard to their own desires. Now they are worried that they are
once again falling victim to a great-power game that resembles
chess, in the sense that the pawns are just sacrificed by the big
players if it serves their long-term geostrategic interests.

For these reasons, the Europeans, on their own, cannot secure
the necessary geostrategic balance between Russia and Europe.

As a former prime minister of a small European country, let me say bluntly: While I appreciate the political cooperation between large and small countries in the EU, it is, seen from a small country's perspective, by far preferable that the necessary geostrategic balance in Europe is secured by a distant, benign, democratic superpower that rises above the intra-European quarrels and political and historical entanglements rather than being entwined in them. Only the United States can exercise that role. It is entirely fair to demand a greater contribution to the common security by Europeans themselves. But at the end of the day, only the United States has the necessary strength, decisiveness, and credibility to counter the Russian assertiveness and uphold the vision of a Europe whole, free, and at peace. That's how it has been since the transatlantic alliance, NATO, was created in 1949, and so it remains.

And it would be in America's own interest not to outsource the job of maintaining the regional power balance to local actors but to stay engaged in European security. First, it would counter fundamental American interests if Russia succeeded in expanding its sphere of influence, destabilizing Europe and threatening the international order. Second, an American disengagement from Europe would risk disintegrating the continent as European countries would struggle to find a cohesive approach to a resurgent Russia. The United States has a vital interest in keeping Europe as a solid, unified partner. And third, the United States has a strong interest in cultivating European allies that welcome and anticipate American leadership and security guaranties, and in return are ready to provide support for the American global policeman.

There will always be a need for a strong power or constellation of powers to prevent conflicts, deter aggression, and protect and maintain an international rules-based order. The key question is whether we want to live in a bipolar or multipolar world with an alliance of repressive states working together to deny their peoples' legitimate demands for change—which is what the balance of power ultimately means. Or do we want a unipolar world with strong and determined leadership by one liberal democratic power assisted by a network of like-minded allies and partners?

The latter option is also a kind of power balance, but a power balance that favors freedom, a power balance that is not static but dynamic and allows freedom to flourish. It is the difference between a city run by rival mobs of gangsters, keeping the peace by agreeing that only one mob will be allowed to terrorize each district, and a city run according to the law, where the peace is kept because the police make sure that people keep it.

We need a superpower that is willing to use its supremacy for the good of all, not just its own good—a supremacy that is so compelling that autocrats, rogue states, or terrorist organizations are discouraged from challenging freedom and peace and deterred from threatening the international order based on the rule of law. Uniquely in history, that is the role the United States has played for the last seventy years. We need it still.

———

BECAUSE OF OUR inherent self-doubt, the world's liberal democracies require true statesmen at the helm to reinforce our belief in our own values and our will to lead on the international stage. In no political office is statesmanship more crucial than in the presidency of the United States. Being the leader of the free world, undertaking the role as the world's policeman, and assuming determined global leadership are daunting tasks that place great demands on conduct, communication, and conviction. In order to perform these tasks efficiently, and in a confident, inspiring, and inclusive manner, the president of the United States must master many different disciplines. Let me just mention three elements in a blueprint for smart international presidential leadership.

First, lead by example. There must be a clear link between the words and deeds of the United States. A red line is a red line that cannot be crossed without consequences. International rules and standards should be not only invoked but also enforced.

The United States should be the unequivocal leader when it comes to respect for and observance of fundamental civil rights and liberal democratic principles, and it must set a good example. Alleged US violations of these fundamental values in Guantánamo and the Abu Ghraib prison, in the CIA's use of torture, and in the NSA's surveillance of American and foreign citizens are weakening the struggle for liberal democracy and fueling anti-Americanism. The next president must make sure that such abuses cannot recur, to rebuild international faith in America's adherence to its own standards.

It is impossible to overstate the damage these abuses have caused to America's global standing. Because of them, the United States has lost the moral high ground; it has lost the weight that allowed it to criticize autocratic regimes for their use of torture and espionage. "What about the NSA?" has become the rallying cry of all those accused by the United States of cyber crime, espionage, and abuses of human rights. Because of them, too, America's image in the eyes of key allies, especially Germany, has been critically injured. Rebuilding the world's trust in American values will demand enormous courage and conviction, and take an immense and long-lasting effort, but it must be done. American leadership is strongest when other countries follow its lead wholeheartedly. The series of scandals has truly broken the hearts of many devoted supporters of America throughout the world.

Most important, leading by example means nurturing and maintaining the American people's commitment to military strength and an active role for the United States in the world. The president has a crucial role to play in constantly and vigorously communicating the need for American global leadership to American voters. If the president fails in this role, it will be tempting for opportunistic politicians in Congress to target defense spending in potentially harmful ways.

The American taxpayer is already bearing the heavy burden of financing the world's largest and most powerful military. Today, the United States accounts for 34 percent of total global investment in defense. It is unmatched, and I will not, as a European, give advice to the American people about whether defense spending should be raised or lowered. But we know that emerging powers are increasing their defense spending, and it is in America's interest to uphold a global reach and maintain the ability to negotiate and facilitate political solutions from a position of strength.

Second, go together, not alone. The next president will need to make building, maintaining, and using alliances a central part of his or her mandate. The president should seek multilateral action as the default option in international operations and, in particular, make good use of already existing, tried and tested alliances and partnerships. While the United States would be able to go it alone in most political, military, and economic actions, building coalitions provides legitimacy, and using existing alliances will often prove the most cost-effective way of doing business.

America's oldest and strongest security alliance is NATO. Since 1949, NATO has been the bedrock of security in the Euro-Atlantic region, and NATO is the framework for consultations and cooperation between allies that share common values and principles: individual liberty, democracy, and the rule of law. This transatlantic alliance is a community of values. Within NATO, the United States has its go-to partners when push comes to shove. The American president should nurture that transatlantic bond.

Operation Unified Protector in Libya demonstrated that NATO is uniquely positioned to respond quickly and effectively to international crises. Besides the United States, only NATO can provide the common command structure and capabilities to plan and execute complex operations. By contrast, ad hoc coalitions, "coalitions of the willing," have no common command structure or capabilities to quickly integrate national forces into a cohesive campaign, nor do they have a standing political forum for debating, and then deciding on, an agreed course of action. Such ad hoc coalitions therefore almost always rely disproportionately on a single nation to bear the brunt of security burdens that ideally should be more equally shared, and there is less transparency and less political control.

In the run-up to the Libyan operation, some countries hesitated to place NATO in charge of a military action, fearing that the alliance would not garner enough support in the region; but it turned out that Arab states preferred to work through NATO. Several of them had already participated in NATO-led operations in Kosovo and Afghanistan, and others had fostered closer relations with NATO through partnership programs. Yet when the air campaign started on March 19, 2011, it was not as a NATO operation but as a coalition of the willing. It was not until the United States clearly stated that it would withdraw from the mission after the initial operations unless NATO took the lead that the skeptics realized that they had to accept a handover of the operation to NATO. This example demonstrates that it takes American leadership to use NATO to its full potential.

There will always be some arguments against using the alliance, in particular because decision making requires consensus, so any member state can block any decision. But experience shows that there is a strong consensual spirit within the alliance and an ability to move quickly when needed, as the Libyan example demonstrates.

Moreover, for an American president, time is spent more effectively building consensus within NATO than building a new costly coalition of the willing, and in a longer-term perspective, smart American global leadership must put emphasis on nurturing already existing alliances. After all, if allies are not cultivated on a daily basis, they may not be there when needed. It is like limbs: If they are not used, they will gradually lose strength. For effective execution of security operations, the American president should think NATO first.

It may appear that NATO is largely a tool to be used in Europe, especially in these times of growing Russian aggression, but it is worth remembering that NATO's largest and longest-ever deployment was in Afghanistan, thousands of miles away, while the Libyan operation was also conducted outside Europe. NATO already has partnerships with Australia, New Zealand, Japan, and South Korea, among other countries; those partnerships could, and should, be strengthened, and the United States should take the lead in doing so.

Alliances are especially important when it comes to the time-consuming and expensive job of rebuilding and stabilizing former conflict zones.

Military operations should be accompanied and followed up by a comprehensive approach involving twenty-first-century Marshall Plans for the reconstruction of devastated societies to prevent failed states and breeding grounds for extremism and terrorism. Any military operation should have such a plan—an "Operation Wealth of Nation," so to speak—embedded in it, and strong alliances are crucial in order to finance and sustain these long-term engagements.

Third, the future president will need to use personal diplomacy. The president must act as the visible leader of the free world. He or she must "lead the leaders," acting as first among equals in the community of democracies, and, as far as possible, a friend among friends. This will mean building good personal relationships with leaders of the liberal democracies, including frequent visits to those allied liberal democracies and outreach to media and opinion formers all over the free world. And the president must exercise predictability, reliability, and commitment to allies and a firm stance against opponents—that is, keep promises and make sure there will be no crossing of red lines.

As prime minister of Denmark, I saw the value of personal diplomacy and support from the American president. At the beginning of 2006, I needed American backing to calm the waters in the Muslim world in the wake of the "cartoon crisis." A Danish newspaper had published some cartoons depicting the prophet Mohammed. Eventually it led to violent protests in a number of Muslim countries, culminating in attacks on the Danish embassies in Syria, Lebanon, and Iran. The initial public reaction from Washington at the subordinate State Department level was ambiguous, and interpreted as criticism of the cartoons, probably because the State Department found it distracting that the cartoons stirred up anti-Western sentiment among Muslims while the United States was struggling to improve the image of America in the Muslim world. However, taking the close relationship between Denmark and the United States into account, that lack of clear support for the Danish government was disappointing. Political parties in parliament also started to question the heavy Danish engagement in international military operations, including Afghanistan, if we couldn't rely on our allies in such a critical situation. I concluded that we needed unequivocal American support to put an end to the violence and protect Danish property and interests. The United States had to use its influence to get governments in the region to stop the violence. I decided to call President George W. Bush.

I told the president that many Arab countries seemed to have difficulties controlling the extremist opposition. The pressure was building up, and threats were being issued against Danes and Danish property. I urged him to let the leaders of those countries know that America would not tolerate threats to Denmark and Danish interests. The president expressed his support and solidarity. There was no doubt in his mind: The United States would stand up for a strong ally and a good friend, and he promised to use America's clout to help calm the situation in the region. American diplomats started working actively with the governments of Muslim countries, they managed to pour oil on troubled waters, and gradually the protests faded away.

This is just one tiny example of the significance of American global leadership. For my country, a small nation of 5.6 million inhabitants, the backing of the world's superpower in a crisis like this was of vital importance. When warranted, the leader of the free world must stand ready to engage personally, and possibly help other leaders of liberal democracies, irrespective of the size of the nation. Effective leadership and conduct is also a matter of taking a principled stance, and being a friend who can be trusted.

―――――

WE WHO ENJOY the privilege of living in free societies have an interest, and I would say an obligation, to promote freedom and democracy in the world. This was the driving force behind the Freedom Agenda that President George W. Bush launched, most powerfully, in his second inaugural speech on January 20, 2005: "The survival of liberty in our land increasingly depends on the success of liberty in other lands. The best hope for peace in our world is the expansion of freedom in all the world. . . . So it is the policy of the United States to seek and support the growth of democratic movements and institutions in every nation and culture, with the ultimate goal of ending tyranny in our world." It has been called an idealistic foreign policy, and set up as a contrast to the so-called realistic foreign policy, but there is no contradiction. Yes, it is idealistic, because we regard human rights as universal, but it is also realistic because increasing freedom and democracy is the best way to improve our own security. Democracies are more peaceful than dictatorships.

President Bush emphasized Japan on several occasions as an example of a successful transformation from an authoritarian militaristic state to a peaceful democracy. By creating a Japanese democracy after 1945 and making sure that it could not be overturned before it had taken root, the United States managed to turn a foe into an ally. Countless times, President Bush mentioned Germany, South Korea, and Eastern Europe as examples illustrating that freedom and democracy can turn former enemies into friends and allies. And why should a similar transformation not be possible in today's dictatorships?

In this context, the United Nations *Arab Human Development Report* from 2002 was an eye-opener. The report, which was prepared by Arab experts, revealed how the Arab countries are lagging behind in crucial areas, due to three deficits: a deficit of freedom, a deficit of education, and a deficit of women's empowerment and participation in public life. Subsequent reports have, by and large, confirmed that these deficits persist; and while some progress has been made since 2002, there is no doubt that tyranny and oppression in the Middle East have led to anger and resentment. Feeling powerless and frustrated, many people have turned to extremist religious leaders. That has, in turn, provided fertile ground for recruiting terrorists.

President Bush took the mantle of leadership with his Freedom Agenda. He launched a number of initiatives to promote freedom and democracy in the region. In June 2002 he officially launched the idea of a two-state solution, with Israel and a democratic Palestine living side by side in peace and security. Peace negotiations began on this basis; elections were held in Palestine, and later, moreover, in Lebanon. The Freedom Agenda made progress, but as so often is the case, the militant forces and terrorists in the region succeeded in stopping the promising development. However, that is not an argument against the promotion of freedom and democracy but rather a reinforcement of the fact that it requires considerable strength and determination to win the fight against tyranny and terror.

In free elections, you obviously run the risk that extreme forces can win seats in parliament. Indeed, we have seen such examples. That has led some skeptics to warn that too much freedom can lead to instability and chaos. But we cannot, out of convenience, sacrifice freedom and democracy to maintain order and oppression. In the long run, dictatorship leads to rebellion. No ruler can endlessly suppress the will of the people. No people can forever be held in serfdom. No power is stronger than man's legitimate demand for freedom. In the long run, freedom and democracy are the best guarantees of peace, security, and stability.

Nevertheless, there are people who prefer stability and order to freedom and democracy. They argue that democracy is not the solution for extremely complex societies with deep-rooted tribal traditions. When Mu'ammar Gadhafi, Hosni Mubarak, and Saddam Hussein were toppled, it opened a Pandora's box of religious, ethnic, and political strife. Their countries plunged into chaos and extremism, which has led some people to conclude that we should show some restraint in all that talk about freedom; that some people are not suited for democracy; that stability must take precedence over freedom; and that a firm hand and some oppression are needed to prevent instability and disorder.

I refuse to accept the basic premise that some people are incapable of democracy and should therefore be condemned to live in tyranny and be deprived of their fundamental freedoms. In fact, I think such an attitude is a manifestation of a repulsive and contestable political and cultural patronage. By what right can we, who enjoy the fruits of free societies, deny other people the same opportunities? We saw the universal desire for liberty in the millions of Iraqis who faced down the terrorists to cast their ballots and elected a free government under a democratic constitution; the millions of Afghans who lined up to vote for the first democratic government in the long history of their country; the Lebanese people who took to the streets to demand their freedom and help drive Syrian forces out of their country; the Tunisian people who toppled a dictator and elected a new parliament and a president in free and fair elections; and the Egyptian people who demanded the overthrow of the dictator Mubarak and the introduction of freedom and democracy.

These young democracies are far from perfect, and in Egypt we have seen a return to authoritarian military rule. However, the problem is not a lack of desire for freedom but rather the lack of a solid democratic culture within weak institutions and fragile societies that are vulnerable to terrorism and rogue armed groups. It is crucial to understand that democracy is much more than elections and majority rule. A true democracy is also about safeguarding individual liberty, protecting the rights of minorities, and securing the rule of law; and an integral part of a true democracy is a vibrant civil society and stable, reliable institutions. It will take time and a lot of effort to develop that political culture. We who live in free societies should remember that it took generations—and sometimes violent conflicts—to develop our democracies. We tend to be too impatient in expecting the emerging democracies to transform into fully fledged democracies overnight. Culture matters, but culture can also be changed. Yes, it may take some time. And we cannot afford to have any more illusions: The forces of oppression will always try to wear freedom down. That is why the forces of freedom must unite under the leadership of the world's strongest liberal democracy.

———

MANY OF US are inclined to believe that the community of values with the best story will win, that the West won the Cold War because the better worldview triumphed, and that progress is inevitable. However, the rise of autocratic powers and Islamic radicalism reminds us that the victory of democratic powers over oppression is not inevitable and it need not be lasting. History has taught us that we cannot be complacent.

Thomas Jefferson reminded us that "the price of liberty is eternal vigilance." I will continue dreaming of the predominance of liberal democracy. I will not accept the argument that certain people are not well suited for democracy. In a world that grows in freedom and democracy, people will have a chance to raise their families and live in peace and build a better future.

The terrorists will lose their recruits and lose their sponsors and lose safe havens from which to launch new attacks, and there will be less room for tyranny and terror. But to ensure the progress of freedom and democracy, we must ensure an invincible global balance in favor of liberal forces. The world's democracies must rise to the challenge, and America must exercise determined global leadership.

Acknowledgments

I really wanted this to be a book of my own. I have therefore limited the number of people who have helped to produce it. But on the other hand, you cannot write such a book without good, professional help from various sides.

First and foremost, I would like to thank our son, Henrik. Throughout, he has been a driving force who has held me to the project, even when I was close to giving up on the idea. Despite having a busy life as an entrepreneur and as the father of a young family, he took the time to help me with good advice and, sometimes, with specific formulations. Henrik is married to an American, Kristina, who lives in the Midwest, and some years ago he became a US citizen. With his Danish upbringing and American background, he has been an ideal sparring partner. I soon found out that Henrik is more versed in American culture and history than many native-born Americans, and I look forward to following his future endeavors to strengthen transatlantic ties.

Next, I would like to thank my English editor, Ben Nimmo. As a non-native English speaker, I needed a native Englishman to edit my English texts. Ben has performed this work in a breathtaking and linguistically balanced manner.

I would also like to thank Michael Ulveman, CEO of Ulveman & Boersting. Michael worked as my press adviser, first when I was prime minister of Denmark and then at NATO. With his unique background, he was able to refresh my memory of some of the experiences I've been through.

My thanks also go to Niels Martin Andersen of Rasmussen Global, who has been my Danish research assistant, and Katie Burkhart of the Harvard Kennedy School, who has been my American research assistant. They have been tireless in their efforts to satisfy my wishes. In this context, I would also like to thank the following institutions for their good cooperation: the Missouri History Museum Library and Research Center and the Harry S. Truman Presidential Library and Museum.

I would also like to thank Ambassador Nicholas Burns, of the Harvard Kennedy School, who twice in 2015 invited me to stay at Harvard University as a Fisher Family Fellow. I got a lot of inspiration from these visits, both from meetings with faculty members, and from my meetings with students.

Of course, I would also like to thank Adam Bellow, of Broadside Books. Since our lunch at Harvard in the fall of 2015, Adam has been a great inspiration who has made numerous suggestions that hopefully have improved the book. Also, many thanks to my American book agent, David M. Larabell, of Creative Artists Agency, who has been instrumental in getting the book published.

Finally, let me thank the rest of my family, for their patience while I focused on the book: our daughter Maria, who has taken charge of Rasmussen Global as chief operating officer; our daughter Christina, who finalized her essay on Ukraine for the Copenhagen Business School while I wrote the book; and my wife, Anne-Mette, who—as always—has borne her discomfort patiently.

It goes without saying that despite all the good advice I have received from my helpers, I bear the responsibility for all analyses and conclusions.

About the Author

ANDERS FOGH RASMUSSEN has been at the center of European and global politics for three decades. He served as the prime minister of Denmark from 2001 until 2009, when he was elected secretary-general of NATO, a position he occupied until September 2014. Rasmussen is currently the director of Rasmussen Global, a geopolitical and security strategic consultancy. A passionate runner, kayaker, and cyclist, he is married and has three children and six grandchildren. He lives in Denmark.